Pursuing THE DREAM

PHOTOGRAPHS BY **STEPHEN SHAMES**

TEXT BY **KATHY GOETZ WOLF**

PREFACE BY **MICHAEL JORDAN**

INTRODUCTION BY **ROGER ROSENBLATT**

APERTURE / FAMILY RESOURCE COALITION / OUTSIDE THE DREAM FOUNDATION

PURSUING THE DREAM

WHAT HELPS CHILDREN AND THEIR FAMILIES SUCCEED

THIS PROJECT WAS
MADE POSSIBLE BY
GENEROUS SUPPORT FROM

THE FORD FOUNDATION
AND
THE CHARLES STEWART MOTT
FOUNDATION

Parents pick up their children from John Marshall
Elementary School in San Diego, California. At John
Marshall, administrators, teachers, support staff, and
parents together plan the school's academic, social,
and staff development programs to create a better
environment for children to learn.

TO MY SON JOSH,
MY GODSONS MARTIN AND AIVAO,
MY NIECE ELIZABETH,
AND MY NEPHEWS THOMAS, ALEX,
ZACH, ALEC, AND STEWART.

Kids and mentors from Friends of the Children
in Portland, Oregon, play touch football.

CONTENTS

A senior citizen from the Center for Intergenerational Learning in Philadelphia mentors sixth graders at school. The center also sponsors an intergenerational theater group, a kids corps of volunteers who do household chores for homebound elders, a literacy/citizenship project for elderly immigrants, and other programs.

The Chicago Bulls feel that it's our responsibility to be actively involved in programs that improve the quality of life in our community. That's why the Bulls' charity arm, CharitaBulls, donated $5 million to help construct the James Jordan Boys & Girls Club and Family Life Center, located two blocks from the United Center on Chicago's West Side. Several members of the Chicago Bulls, including Michael Jordan and Dennis Rodman, have made individual donations and pledges to support the Club's programming.

The James Jordan center, which is a division of Boys & Girls Clubs of Chicago, opened in November of 1996. In addition to offering the types of social, recreation, and physical education opportunities for children and youth for which Boys & Girls Clubs are known, the center also provides services such as day care, computer classes, employment services, and health care for thousands of West Side families. The center is intended to be a safe, nurturing environment for the children of Chicago's inner city, and to serve as an advocate for the rebuilding of America's families. There children and adults alike can come together to learn, socialize, exercise, and find comfort, support, and opportunities that otherwise would not be available.

The Chicago Bulls are proud to be part of the effort to strengthen our community and provide opportunities for its children and families. We truly feel that the James Jordan Boys & Girls Club and Family Life Center exemplifies the theme of this book: providing community-based programs that can help children and their families find happiness and success.

THE CHICAGO BULLS

PREFACE

JAMES JORDAN BOYS & GIRLS CLUB AND FAMILY LIFE CENTER

MICHAEL JORDAN AND THE CHICAGO BULLS

Of everything I've accomplished in life, nothing is more important to me than my family. My wife, Juanita, and I look at our children and we're constantly reminded of how very blessed we are.

I see myself as an example of the difference a strong family and a strong community can make. My parents worked hard to steer me and my brothers and sisters in the right direction. I benefited from teachers, coaches, and neighbors in my community who provided a positive influence for me.

I was also part of the Boys & Girls Club in my hometown of Wilmington, North Carolina. It was where I first learned what it means to work with and respect others. Clubs are places where kids can get involved in activities that will help them learn new skills and get a taste of success. As an adult, I continue to support Boys & Girls Clubs and, particularly, the James Jordan Boys & Girls Club and Family Life Center in Chicago.

The James Jordan center is one of the first Boys & Girls Clubs in the country to be built with the entire family in mind. The James Jordan center is not only a place for kids, it is also a place for parents and other people in the community to find the encouragement and skills they need to reach their dreams.

A quote from my father is on the wall as you walk in the center. He said, "My family is my life." Helping to build this center is my way of showing appreciation for my dad. This is my payback. My father would have been happy and honored to have this club named for him.

In this book, you'll see programs in other communities that make sure children and families get what they need to succeed. These programs may not have the backing of a major sports franchise or bear the name of a famous family, but they all deserve our support in whatever way we can give it.

MICHAEL JORDAN

Opposite: 15-year-old Kendall goes one-on-one with Marque Reed, a staff member and friend who runs the James Jordan Boys & Girls Club's computer lab. The Club's gym is a small-scale replica of the stadium where the Bulls play, complete with championship banners.

School playground in the Sunset Park
neighborhood of Brooklyn, New York.

DREAM CHILDREN: AN ESSAY

ROGER ROSENBLATT

Henry will not face me. We sit close together on small plastic chairs in a classroom at P.S. 314, an elementary school in the Sunset Park area of Brooklyn, New York, where he works with small children in a summer camp. Our knees, drawn high because we are sitting on the low chairs, almost touch, yet he angles his body so that he shows me only his profile. If he turns toward me briefly and catches my eye, he will turn away again at once and gaze out the large schoolroom window at other teenagers languishing on a stoop across the street.

His neighborhood, Sunset Park, consists of approximately 115,000 people, most of them poor, with a median income of $10,200. A quarter of the residents have incomes below the poverty line. They represent a variety of backgrounds: Puerto Rican, African-American, Dominican, Mexican, Jordanian, Pakistani, Chinese, Korean, and Vietnamese. These groups are the latest to populate Sunset Park. They follow the Irish, Finns, Swedes, Norwegians, Poles, and Italians of the late nineteenth century, and the Greeks, Russians, and Jews of the early twentieth. The first area residents were the Dutch and the English, who established farms where the Canarsie Indians had fishing stations before them.

A little over a mile wide and 2.6 miles long, the area lies between blue-collar Bay Ridge to the south, and gentrified Park Slope to the north. The rectangle of the neighborhood slopes down from the high ridge at Eighth Avenue to the east, to Upper New York Bay, where the Statue of Liberty rises. At the top of the ridge is Sunset Park itself, an eighteen-acre public park with old trees and a WPA swimming pool. On the grid of narrow streets and wide avenues between the ridge and the bay lie two- and three-story brownstones with attractive cornices; brick-and-masonry houses with little gardens in the front, where corn is sometimes grown; and many rows of drab no-color tenements. Henry lives in one of these. His home is near Third Avenue, which is close to the water, and is shadowed by the Gowanus Expressway, one of the highways built by Robert Moses to carry white people away from places like Sunset Park.

Henry is sixteen, tall for his age, at about six-feet-one. His skin is a dull, dark brown; antiperspirant under his arms foams white against it. His hair is spun into curlicues. He rarely smiles, though when he does, he looks warm and welcoming in contrast to his usual self-concealing blankness. He is sleepy this morning. He yawns frequently, and fully, his mouth wide open like a baby's. "What else have you seen?" I ask him. He is talking about life on the streets. He has just told me about drug dealers throwing bowling balls and frozen chickens off the roof at police cars. He tells me about a man who held a gun to his head, because he wanted Henry's "fronts," the gold caps he was wearing on his teeth. He tells me about "ho's" doing tricks on his block, kids smoking "blunts," or crack cigars, and the "crews," the gangs.

He tells me about an eleven-year-old boy who was "kind of slow." One afternoon the boy began shaking the bars on his fourth-story window when they came loose. He fell head first into the courtyard and died where Henry was playing.

"What else have you seen?"

"I seen a man throw a telephone out the window, and it hit a baby in a carriage. It nearly killed her. So her father ran up the stairs, and he grabbed the man who threw the phone, and he cut him." He traces a line across his throat with his index finger. "He lived, but he's got this necklace now."

"Did you know the men involved?" I ask him.

"I knew the man who threw the phone," he says. "He's my mother's boyfriend."

"Why did he do that?"

"He was drunk, crazy." He shrugs to indicate that the behavior is normal for his mother's boyfriend. "What did you do when the baby's father slit his throat?" I ask. "I was happy," says Henry. "I laughed when he did it. I even testified against the boyfriend in court. My mother was mad. She's always mad at me." He gives me a glance, then turns his head to the side. "That was when things really blew up at home. So I went to the Center for Family Life and told Jennifer.

"She's been everything to me," he says without emotion. "She makes me think about what I do."

"What about your mother?" I ask him.

"She screams. Says I'm the Devil. Calls me retarded. She says I'm bad. I am bad." He holds his head down. "I hang out. I write up, you know? Do graffiti. I fight, maybe less now, but I used to fight all the time. A crew attacked me. I hit one of them in the head with a baseball bat. Put him in intensive care. When I start fighting, it's like seek and destroy. You start with me and you're the enemy. Nobody else in sight. You my spotlight, my way out. You the exit door."

"The exit door from what?" I ask him. He does not answer. "Are other grown-ups in your life good to you?" I ask him. "Teachers?"

"Some are okay," he says. "I had a teacher tell me: 'I don't give a shit if you come to class or not. I get paid anyway.'"

"Police?"

"When I got arrested for writing up, a woman cop told me she hopes they send me to jail."

"Ministers? Priests?" I ask. He shakes his head. "I don't have religion."

"The Mayor? The Governor? The President?" I am speaking a foreign language. "Are there any grown-ups who help you?" I ask him.

"Jennifer," he says softly. "People at the Center."

The Center for Family Life, the social service agency in which Henry is a client, has served Sunset Park for eighteen years. It was founded by, and is headed by, two Sisters of the Good Shepherd, Mary Paul and Geraldine, though it is not a Catholic institution, and is run for people of all faiths or of none. The Center operates on the principle that family life represents the strength of a community, and that social work must attend to every member of a troubled family, and to every facet of life in a neighborhood. Thus, besides counseling, the Center's operations include an employment agency, an emergency food program, a thrift shop, advocacy and legal services, a theater program, a literacy program, summer camps, day care for both small children and for school-age children, and a neighborhood foster care program that is becoming a model for the country. In a neighborhood foster care program, the foster families are selected within the community of the original family, so that the children do not lose touch with their homes.

The Center is located on 43rd Street, between Third and Fourth avenues, in a yellowish three-story building honeycombed with counseling rooms and play areas. The staff is made up of about fifty part-time aides, mostly young people in the neighborhood, and twenty full-time social workers, like Jennifer Zanger, who works with Henry, and Julie Stein Brockway, who directs the theater program.

I sit with Mary Paul and Geraldine in the Center's "Family Room," a combination living room and conference room in which the staff members meet with families who seek the Center's help. Geraldine is in her early fifties. She is tall, robust, and she laughs a lot; she strides through the neighborhood streets bellowing greetings to seemingly everyone. "Isn't she beautiful!" she says about a little girl who waves to her. "Aren't they wonderful!" she says about the staff. Mary Paul is in her late seventies. She is hardly five feet tall, and she has the face of a meditative doll. Her voice is staticky and childlike, a little like the actress Meg Tilley's. More studious than Geraldine, she spends time reading philosophy and religious tracts, and she watches the news like a hawk. The nuns are opposite in temperament, identical in attitude, and equally formidable when it comes to fighting for a client, or for funding for the Center. I once mentioned the two of them to Mario Cuomo, when he was Governor of New York, and thus a perpetual target of their irritation and of their relentless demands for more and better services. He rolled his eyes toward heaven. "Oh, them!" he said.

Yet government is beginning to catch on to the value of community-based programs. In late December 1996, New York's mayor Rudolph Giuliani announced a plan that called for the decentralization of the child-welfare bureaucracy, and included such ideas as neighborhood foster care and local networks. The basic idea of neighborhood structures is already in place in Los Angeles and other cities.

"Why do you think that families hurt children?" I ask Mary Paul.

"I think it all comes down to certain vulnerabilities in human nature," she says. "People do have positive goals in regard to children. But somehow these goals become subverted because, paradoxically, people become overcommitted to them. Life ceases to be an adaptation and an exchange with an outside environment. We become mere doers. We do and we do and we do, and we grow to be more narrowly focused and more narrowly driven. Soon we lose energy, and we fail. It's the law of entropy."

"Does that happen in education?" I ask.

"Absolutely," she says. "A few years ago, schools in places like New York started out being attentive to the needs of children in a multicultural environment. Perfectly sensible, given all the new immigrant groups who were coming in. Then people became overcommitted to that one goal of multiculturalism. They forgot about what else was worthwhile in education. They thought that education was about self-esteem."

"Or take reading," says Geraldine. "Schools get so concerned with proving that children are taught to read, they lose sight of the rest of education. The pressure on teachers to demonstrate that students can read is so great these days, that's all they focus on. They forget that a whole child is in front of them."

"Special education started out as a result of lawsuits to give more individualized attention to handicapped children. So what has it become? Bigger and bigger and wealthier and more closed in on itself. Once you get a child certified into Special Ed in New York City, it takes the king's horses to get the child extracted."

"How does your observation about narrow goals apply to foster care?" I ask them.

"The reason we instituted neighborhood foster care," says Geraldine, "is that child welfare in this country, the Child Welfare Administration in particular, focuses only on the well-being of the child. Not the child as an extension of the parent, and certainly not the parent as an extension of the child. Not on the family environment nor on the community environment but on the child alone."

"The way foster care is practiced around the country," says Mary Paul, "is to remove the child from the original family as far away as possible. Often the taking of children is done abruptly. A child is removed by the CWA from school because it's easier than confronting the mother.

"If a boy like Henry had to go into foster care, how would it help him to be removed far away from the mother he is so desperate to know? How would it help her? Sometimes children are removed in the middle of the night, with the police in attendance. They'll use even more coercive methods. I cannot stand the violence of it. Violence affects me physically. I have no tolerance for it. I find an enormous amount of psychological cruelty in conventional foster care, and I can't abide it."

"This is why the Center began neighborhood foster care in Sunset Park," says Geraldine. "We've been doing this seven years now, and sometimes we succeed and sometimes not. But even the failures can be a partial success. A child whom we placed in foster care here has a mother who is seriously mentally ill. The woman will stand in the street and scream up at the windows of the little girl's foster parents' house. She will sit in the hallway and bang on the door with her fists all night. And she will not go for treatment. And still the little girl, because she has been allowed to remain close to her mother, sees the disease for what it is. She understands. It doesn't make the mother well, but it helps the girl. And now her father, whom we are also working with, and who left the mother long ago, is slowly beginning to assume responsibilities for his daughter."

"To maintain the basic connections," says Mary Paul, "to maintain the child's environment no matter how terrible part of it may be, it is so important. The child is removed to a new home. But the child also remains in the same neighborhood, attends the same school, keeps the same friends."

"So overcommitment as applied to the Child Welfare Administration means focusing excessively on the injured child?" I ask.

"Yes," says Mary Paul. "It isn't that they do not care about the child. But they care about the child out of context, removed from all that matters to the child."

"Are the police and the courts overcommitted to a particular vision of children?" I ask.

"The police and the court system have to be committed to a vision of law and order," says Mary Paul. "That's their social assignment, and their duty. Citizens tell them that more and more these days. And in a rigid view of things, that's as it should be. But when a policeman and a judge only see a child through the prism of law and order, they are not addressing a human being."

I ask: "What about the child who is a rapist or a murderer?"

"For them it's too late. They have to be seen as criminals. They are criminals," says Mary Paul. "But Henry spraying graffiti on a building wall? Or even Henry using a baseball bat in a street fight. Henry is not a criminal, not yet. He is a child in need of help and attention. People in charge of an orderly society sometimes have to look at the world from the child's point of view."

"And the government?" I ask. "When funds are withdrawn from schools or child welfare organizations like yours, or from any institutions that serve children, is that because of too narrow a focus?"

"In a way," says Mary Paul. "All one reads these days is how strapped city, state, and federal budgets are. Politicians win points by coming up with ways to save the country money. We have to reduce the deficit. We have to reduce the national debt. For whose benefit should we rescue the economy? It is always the children and the grandchildren. Yet how should we save the economy?"

"Take money away from children," Geraldine offers, and laughs.

"Exactly," says Mary Paul. "Take the money from the children even though you are focusing on the children as the reason for rescuing the economy. By this logic, you will amass a fortune as a legacy, and at the same time, kill off the legatees."

"What about individual parents?" I ask them.

"When parents fail their children," says Mary Paul, "it is almost always because of an overcommitment to one or another vision of a child."

"Henry's mother only yells at him and degrades him," says Geraldine, "because she thinks that's how to make him toe the mark. And naturally Henry is angry at her. He's in a constant rage. And he takes out his rage in street fights."

"A parent says, 'I want my child to be good and respectful and therefore I have a right to beat him,'" says Mary Paul. "Or a parent will get focused on something other than the child, which is theoretically supposed to be in the child's best interests. But it hurts the child. It's not unlike the government.

"This is a poor neighborhood. Money drives much of people's behavior. In a Dominican family that we failed to help, the father could not find work in New York so he went to work in Buffalo, and he returned every four weeks or so with money for his wife and his six-year-old daughter. He was working six days a week up there, and nights, too, and he was saving the money all by himself. And when he'd come home, his wife would greet him at the door with: 'How much do you have? It's not enough. You're stupid. You're lazy.' So the little girl picked all that up. And she'd say to her father, 'You're no good.' Finally, one day when he could no longer stand the humiliation he hauled off and whacked the child in the face. The parents' drive, their focus, was to get more money, to provide a better life and a better future. The parents had tunnel vision about earning money. And the daughter got whacked.

"When a goal or a set of goals gets so enclosed, parents will do anything and hurt anybody. The goal is like an amoeba. It takes in food but it does not enter into an exchange with its environment. It merely elaborates itself. It kills itself by excess. The rage of parents who have sacrificed so much and invested so much and then nothing works . . . they begin to see the child as a repudiation of their capacity for giving."

"What about neglect?" I ask.

"Neglect usually comes when a parent gives up," says Geraldine. "There is a goal, then obsessive commitment to that goal, then failure, then surrender. The child is abandoned."

"Or there may be an overcommitment to a vision of the child as a free spirit," says Mary Paul. "The vision of a child as an adult. Just another grown-up in the family. This applies more to wealth-ier parents, I think. They really didn't want the responsibility of rearing a human being; they wanted another witty, charming, urbane grown-up in the house. So neglect was built into their vision of the child in the first place. And, of course, when the child turned out not to be the delightful grown-up companion the parents originally had in mind, but rather a surly little beast, they neglected the child again."

"What happens when a parent assaults or kills a child?" I ask. "How is that a form of overcommitment?"

"You know," says Mary Paul, "the feeling that one has to love a child can be overwhelming, especially for those, and there are many, who do not. And then the child reminds you every day of your inability to build a world for it. It calls forth something that the parent cannot give.

"A Mexican mother in this neighborhood killed her child by repeated beatings. It was in the papers. A family of four. They lived down by the harbor. They had come to America fairly recently. The father worked in a sweatshop, and he was laid off. They were illegals, so they were also in hiding. Afraid of arrest and deportation. Not enough money for rent or food. And the terrible summer heat, that killing heat spell in mid-July.

"And it said in the papers that the family 'somehow made its way from Mexico to Sunset Park.' Somehow made its way! Can you imagine what commitment it took for that family to get from Mexico to here, what ambitions for a new life they had, their dream of America? They wind up in a situation where all forms of love and rationality are abandoned to that dream, which had at its center the children, after all. Here we go again. Everything for the children. And then one day the child becomes a noise. And the noise has to be stilled.

"We have to avoid the closed systems," she says. "Another thing the papers said about that family was that none of their neighbors knew them. They knew nothing about them. It is always that way. Nobody knows anything until it is too late."

"A client of ours killed her daughter," says Geraldine. "The girl was about three-and-a-half. She had diabetes, and she was always thirsty. So she would go to the refrigerator again and again for juice. The mother was very poor, and was unaware that the child had diabetes. She had so little food. She told the girl not to keep going to the refrigerator, but the girl kept going anyway. So the mother hit her in the head, the child went into a coma, and then she died. The mother did not want to kill her little girl, of course. She was thinking about the juice."

Institutions like the Center for Family Life came into being because America, as an institution, has never made a commitment to the context in which children live and function. Community-based programs often derive their achievements from the fact that they deliberately run counter to historical practices. They have to; the history of childhood in America is by and large a history of failure. Statistics and headlines make it appear that American children have never had it as bad as they do today. That may be so, but children have always been mistreated in this country. A newborn infant found lying in a dumpster makes news these days; in mid-nineteenth-century Philadelphia, a newborn was discovered in a garbage can every other day of the week. The trouble that kids get into is no different, either. In Samuel Phillips's *Advice to a Child* (1729), the author warned youth against "fornication." Phillips wrote that it is "too evident by the fruit that this has been much practiced."

The great difference between the present day and the past is that today's children seem to be assaulted from more angles than ever, and all at once. But what they are suffering represents the culmination of a 350-year pattern of ill treatment that began, in almost every instance, with noble intentions about the child and no thought given the family or community.

What Mary Paul observed about the current destructive focus on narrowly conceived goals applies historically as well. In the seventeenth century there was an overcommitment to what was perceived as the depraved nature of the child, and to original sin. In Plymouth Colony, the minister John Robinson argued that all children possessed "a stubbornness, and stoutness of mind arising from natural pride," and that it was the obligation of parents to beat those tendencies down. After that the child would show "humility and tractableness," Robinson said, to which additional virtues would accrue. Modern psychologists theorize that such a crushing of the child's spirit (the afflicted child could have been one or two years old) led to a personal sense of shame and self-doubt. This in turn affected Puritan society at large, in which public humiliations were common. In 1646, "stubborn child laws"

were enacted (though never enforced) in Massachusetts, which provided the death penalty for "a stubborn or rebellious son . . . which shall not obey the voice of his Father or the voice of his Mother."

The idea that a child was an innately disruptive creature who had to be beaten into submission continued into the eighteenth century. The attitude is made plain in the writings of Susanna Wesley, and of her son, John, the founder of the Methodist movement. In a letter to John in 1732, Susanna set out her principles of upbringing, which were formulated to restrain the will of the child. John Wesley's influential educational teaching emerged accordingly: "If you spare the rod, you spoil the child; if you do not conquer, you ruin him. Break his will now and his soul shall live, and he will probably bless you to all eternity." In Sunset Park, Henry's mother shares something of this philosophy.

In the nineteenth century, the idea to which the country became overcommitted was the perfectibility of the child. This was not as abrupt a turnaround from Puritan theology as it might seem, since perfection was the Puritan aim as well. Now, however, the path would be different. By the beginning of the nineteenth century, the English philosopher John Locke (1632–1717) was long gone, but his teaching in "An Essay Concerning Human Understanding" (1690), which was reprinted in 1692 under the title, "Some Thoughts Concerning Education," had enormous influence on American child development. Locke viewed the child's mind not as inherently evil or rebellious, but as a *tabula rasa*. Character derives from knowledge, he said; knowledge from experience. His philosophy was compatible with both the hereditarian and environmental views of intelligence, but its main contribution to American thought was to provide a way of looking at the child as an entity capable of infinite improvement.

Thus, for the first half of the nineteenth century, reformers, physicians, educators, and professional moralists began to see children as creatures in need of structural environments in which all their intellectual and emotional capabilities would receive instruction. Orphanages were set up, as were other houses of refuge, asylums, and schools for infants in factories. In such institutions children would not be whipped into virtue (at least not theoretically), but would be made to use formal learning for moral and social advancement. They would memorize and recite passages from the Bible. They would learn by rote. They would read the approved canon. Literacy was thus extended to the masses, and the masses were subjected to rigid regulation; individual differences among children were to be erased. The stated goal of these reformers was to govern a child's passions by separating intellect from the emotions. Some historians see the emergence of these reformist institutions as an effort to exert dominance over a vast potential work force. They regard the structural innovations that arose from 1790 to 1860 as part of a national strategy to create docile laborers for the new industrialized, urbanized order. Whether or not the new institutions were part of a deliberate effort to quash and regiment the spirit of children, they often did so. Locke's philosophy of the blank slate did not prevent the country from putting children to work for adults, even if they did it in the name of bettering children's lives. At the same time, the systematic effort to establish these institutions and to remove children from what were deemed harmful social influences would eventually end up in the sort of foster care violence that Mary Paul abhors.

In short, the difference between the mid-nineteenth century and the early seventeenth is that the country grew to prefer one kind of child submission to another. The idea that an American child was to be forcibly shaped from something less into something more held fast; it applies today. And some of the old Puritan severity died hard. The Reverend Francis Wayland (1790–1865), a Baptist minister who was also president of Brown University, explained in a published letter how he had starved his fifteen-month-old baby boy into submission, and he recommended his educational procedure to others. By the late nineteenth century the idea of the perfectibility of the child had merged with the idea of the perfectibility of society. Perfectibility had always been present in America's view of itself, and now children were brought into the dream. Juvenile courts developed, primarily as mechanisms for separating children from parents who were considered unfit, especially lower-class immigrants. The state had an ideal of behavior that would help perfect the state. Professionals reformed the school systems in an effort to centralize control of education. The curriculum changed. The new educational leaders were said to have brought about a social order in which education became a form of human engineering. Children still served the labor force. The black children of recently freed slaves continued to be apprenticed to white families, thus maintaining the sub-

stance of slavery. But the major thrust of the country as it entered the twentieth century was that a child should be molded into an ideal American, whatever that was, and that all the new inventive knowledge that enthralled the country at the time could be brought to the task.

The commitment, then, at the beginning of the twentieth century was a commitment to science, hard and soft. A child could be studied, analyzed, directed. Heredity began to be seen as a key element in determining intelligence. IQ testing began in 1916, the hereditarian theory of IQ fitting in conveniently with notions of nativism and with racism. Every aspect of a child's behavior, and of a child's salvation, could be traced to a scientific "cause." G. Stanley Hall's theory that "ontogeny recapitulates phylogeny" became hugely popular, as did other mechanistic views of human activity. The term "adolescence" was coined, thus creating a new scientific category to be observed.

The Progressive reform movement of the early 1900s was driven by the belief that science could perfect America, and that professional expertise was the way to raise standards of education, health, nutrition, and social conduct. One sociologist calls the era that of "professional child-savers." The first White House Conference on Children was held in 1909. Reformers believed that only a hierarchical, centralized authority could serve children properly, and that there should be nationally defined standards of behavior, indeed a nationally defined culture. From 1890 to 1915 the theme was reform; from 1915 to 1930 the theme was professionalism. Every facet of national life, it seemed, was ready to put children under a microscope.

Meanwhile, the government continued its general policy of separating the poor parent and child; children were still to be "saved" from the demoralizing influence of parents. For Native Americans, salvation meant the creation of special boarding schools by the Indian Bureau, whose conditions were so horrendous that a government investigation of federal Indian policy was launched in the late 1920s. Congress passed the Social Security Act in 1935. Title IV, Aid to Dependent Children (A.D.C.), provided help for fatherless families, but the fathers had to remain absent from the home for a family to be eligible for funds. Poor children increasingly became dependents of the state, as many are today, and this group is certain to be made poorer and larger by the 1996 welfare reform act.

Since the 1940s, there has been no government strategy for keeping families together. In 1962, Congress broadened the range of services under A.D.C. to include day-care facilities and work incentives for parents. The aim was to see that parents entered the labor market and that kids got taken care of, but the result was to encourage their separation from one another. Congress has been committed to children's well-being for practically the entire history of the republic, but it has performed poorly. Even the indisputably successful Head Start program (1965), designed to educate children under the age of five, has functioned as a way to free parents to go to work. This is fine for the health of the economy, questionable for that of the family and community. The persistent tendency of government action has been to divide parent and child for the sake of serving the child. Intentionally or not, the government has forced poor parents to choose between their children and the family's financial survival, instead of addressing the wider picture of political and economic reform.

Whether children in America have been seen as born sinners, or as clay to be molded, or as foreigners to Americanize, or as psychological curiosities, or as laboratory animals, or as waifs in distress, the overcommitment to one or another of these views has resulted in failure. For all the attention it has paid to children, the country has yet to develop a comprehensive philosophy about them, much less a coherent, functioning national policy toward families as a whole. Even a superficial survey of the history shows a number of roads pursued that either dead-end or never meet. Some of the roads go in circles. The teaching of religious fundamentalism in the 1970s and 1980s mirrors the fanaticism of the Puritans. A book favored by the "Moral Majority" called *Family Life* (1976), assures the reader that "all children, not just certain children, all children, are born delinquent."

The nineteenth-century English essayist Charles Lamb wrote an essay in 1821 called "Dream-Children: A Reverie." It was about an evening spent by the fire with his children, in which he told them heart-warming tales of their family's history. At the end of the piece, Lamb revealed to the reader with straightforward melancholy that in fact he had no children, that he was unmarried and lived alone, and the whole story had been merely a reverie, a dream. The essay was about what his life had missed.

————————

Observers have suggested that the trouble with much of social work in America is that it, too, has become overcommitted to a goal. American social work began rather informally, creating small community centers for new immigrant groups at the turn of the century. Gradually there developed case work agencies, group work agencies, and larger community-building agencies. Soon a full-fledged profession was formed. Then somewhere between the late 1950s and the early 1970s, the agenda changed. Suddenly all the money and the prestige went to the clinical treatment of individual children. Social work began to zero in on growing street violence and drugs, almost exclusively.

But, as a result of this overcommitment to the clinical treatment of individuals, the original idea of creating and sustaining small communities all but disappeared. The Center for Family Life became one of the few places that still believed in it. And the basis of the belief, especially insofar as children are concerned, is that a child requires an active network of associations to achieve a stable, useful life. If the Center is overcommitted to anything, and the Sisters are so self-conscious of this notion that they continually examine the possibility, it is to this comprehensive and flexible view of the individual functioning in a small, fluid, and interconnected society.

Mary Paul's personal philosophy is that life is to be understood as a journey, that people are to be seen *in via*, on the way. This view of experience as process informs the Center's dealings with the local police, the schools, the politicians, the store owners, the churches, the hospital, even with the gangs. Gang members, or former gang members, have been enlisted in the programs to work with smaller children. At first, parents were leery of this idea, but the gang members took their responsibilities seriously. Parents were invited to observe or participate in the program at any time.

In practice the Center's philosophy comes to teaching that everybody is capable of change for the better, not perfection, and that there may be backslides. The Sisters and the staff members relentlessly remind the children how important they are. Parents, too, are assured of their worth. This is often a more difficult idea to get across to people like Henry's mother, since the wounds of the older people go deeper. Mary Paul calls destructive parents "yesterday's children," some of whom are simply not reclaimable. The Center acknowledges this; the question of the future of Henry's mother is still up in the air. Mary Paul recalls a recent morning when a client phoned in panic because, the night before, her new boyfriend had beaten a friend of hers so badly, the woman was put in the hospital.

"I have no doubt that this man is very dangerous," she says, "that he could seriously harm my client and her little girl, who is four. But the woman wanted to bring the man in here for help, before the police came for him, probably. So here they sat, all three in a row. The little girl pretended to be coloring in a book. The man sat beside my client, who was sitting between him and her child. He was holding my client's hand all the time, and he was very tender with her. At one point she had to leave the room to get some water, and he gathered up the little girl in his arms.

"And then he proceeded to tell me that he felt totally justified in beating up that other woman, because, he said, 'if someone gets in my face, they deserve what I can give them.' And then, as I drew him out little by little, he let me know that his father had abandoned him when he was three, and then, years later, he came back, and this man tangled with him, and, he told me, he 'bashed his head in.' Then his mother gave him up because she preferred to be with her boyfriend. So he bashed her head in as well. I didn't bother to ask for a precise physical description of bashing, but the man said that he had absolutely no compunction about assaulting anybody. He had done so the night before.

"The little girl sat there taking everything in. She was drawing with her crayons, but there was nothing she was going to miss. Meanwhile, the man went on professing 'I love you' to the two of them. One learns that these professions of love are the other side of rage. There's an eroticism that is heightened in rage. Incredible anger turns into an embrace. And vice versa. And the woman kept saying, 'I love you, dear' and 'I know you have suffered,' offering him the defense of victimhood, which can't last very long. And yet the defense is real for him. He could easily, with an old woman like me, crawl into my lap and become a little boy again, and express the cravings of his childhood.

"But make no mistake. He is very dangerous, to both mother and daughter. I think so often of the price that society pays for not taking one such human being and working with him, those forgotten people who were written off and despised."

Mary Paul and Geraldine note that if one is going to see life as a journey, one must concede that the journey can falter. A seventeen-year-old Chinese boy named Tommy is a counselor at summer camp at P.S. 314. He takes his work seriously. And he is liked by the smaller children. But as soon as Tommy leaves the Center's precincts, he goes back to the streets, where he is a follower, not a leader, and where his life is rolling downhill.

Tommy is short and stocky. His crewcut stands up like charred match sticks. He is a smooth talker and a con artist. He blames every element of society for his troubles, except himself. He tells interviewers what he thinks they want to hear.

"America?" he says. "I don't think America cares much about kids. The people you deal with, they stereotype you. The cops stereotype you. If there were more jobs out there, there would be less crime. Less drugs, you know?" He has sold drugs and committed robberies. He has carried a 9mm pistol. He belongs to a gang called FEB, which, he says, stands for "Fuck every bitch" or "Fuck everybody." He recently served time for being present at a murder.

"I didn't do it," he tells me. "My man did, my friend. He stabbed this guy three times in the back because they tried to get our crew. They pulled out hammers. And one of them tried to stab my man with a screwdriver. So my man cut him. I didn't do nothin'. I had a razor on me, but I threw it on the subway tracks. That's how the cops caught me. They got my prints.

"My man got twenty-five years to life. I got three months in Rikers. Rikers ain't no joke." For the first time his expression looks honest, and it is full of fear. "I seen people get sliced. You don't look right, they'll cut you. The COs (correctional officers) sell the prisoners the weapons. There's lots of things you don't know before you seen Rikers. Like people sticking razors in their mouth, or up their ass."

"Is there any adult in your life who has been helpful to you?" I ask him. "Your parents?"

"My mother gets up at five to go to work. Gets home at three in the afternoon. I see her for a few, then I'm out the door. My father left home when I was two. The streets are my father." He seems to enjoy the melodrama of that sentence.

"How about the Center?" I ask

"The Center is great," he says. "It keeps me out of trouble."

"As long as you're in it," I suggest. "But once you're back on the streets?"

"On the streets I live for real," he says. "It's scary. I don't want my life to end soon but it could happen. I could go any time. Vanish. No more." I cannot tell if he's putting me on. "I had a dream," he says. "I was going home looking for my mother. But then I was in a funeral place, and my mother was dead. But then I saw her again, walking like a block away, and I'm calling her, and she doesn't stop walking, but she turns around and waves."

"Did she say anything to you in your dream?" I ask him.

"No," he says. "She just waved goodbye."

It should not be assumed that all the kids who come to the Center are in serious trouble. Marisol, who was born in Puerto Rico and who came here at the age of five, has just turned sixteen. She wears her hair short, carries her body like an athlete, and she talks a blue streak. Her brother is in prison for armed robbery, and her parents have been separated since Marisol was twelve. She misses her father, who lives in Florida, and whom she visits often. Yet she is very close to her mother, a nurse, who is the main moral influence in her life.

"She brought me up right," says Marisol. "And it's hard to do right sometimes, because of peer pressure 'n shit. It's hard to be a kid because of drugs. It's hard to be a girl, because of sex. I don't do drugs because it's bad for me, and I want to live longer. I'm a virgin, because I don't want to have a baby, and I don't want to get AIDs 'n shit.

"There is nothing I'd change in my life right now, except that I wish my dad lived closer. But he's there for me, like 24/7. I've got it good. A kid I took care of last summer used to come every day with his arms black and blue. He'd tell me his mother hit him. I just prayed for him, you know?"

A fourteen-year-old boy from Taiwan named Jimmy reveres his parents, plays basketball, is a straight-A student, and wants to become a stockbroker. He has the deliberately open face of a deadpan comedian.

"What do you do when other kids tell you to put down the books and come out in the streets?" I ask him.

"I just state the facts," says Jimmy. "I tell them why I want to get high grades, what I want to do with my future, stuff like that. They don't call me a Herb. They know who I am."

"Who are you?" I ask him.

"I'm a Chinese kid who has developed a fabulous personality in Brooklyn," he tells me.

Between the contented extremes of Marisol and Jimmy and the endangered extreme of Tommy are most of the Center's kids. Like kids in other places, they are frightened much of the time, are both "cool" and bewildered, and they are furtively observant. The theater group run by staff worker Julie Stein Brockway puts on playlets that involve domestic situations. The dialogue is improvised. In a recent performance, the kids paired off as parent and child, parent and parent, teacher and child, and so forth. In one scene, a girl playing the mother and a boy the father, immediately launched into the following exchange: He: "You take the TV." She: "You take the car." In another scene, a mother tells her son, who has just been arrested: "You are living in your father's world." A magazine put out by the Center contains material that suggests how the children are thinking. A story by an eight-year-old goes: "I like my own game which nobody even knows how to play. The name is The Game to Play. Spin spin, make me dizzy, hypnotize me. You have to move your man, and if you go to the hole you have to kill who you want to kill."

A poem titled "I am the Drug," contains these lines:

I am the one who has taken you to prison.
I have made you the woman that you are now.
I have you bend down and you are in love with me.
There is no one on earth who can come between our love.

To all these children the Center brings the message that a child is part of a family, a family part of a community. It strives to keep Jimmy and Marisol on course. It is not fooled by kids like Tommy, and it will wait for such time as Tommy decides that he does not want to fool himself. For the most part, the Center exists for people like Henry, who straddle the two available worlds of defeat and survival. Henry's mother tells him that he is bad. Jennifer Zanger tells him the opposite.

"I try to be as straight as I can," Jennifer says. "In the beginning I'm nonjudgmental. But eventually I am quite judgmental. What's wrong is wrong. The thing is to judge the behavior, not the person. I've said to Henry many times: 'Do you want to go to jail? Do you think that you deserve to be in jail?' When he says yes, he means that 'a person like me deserves to be in jail.' That's how he's been made to think of himself. So much of this stuff is having a picture of who you could be, or of who you are. One of the best things about the Center, because it's service-oriented, is that teens get to work with kids who adore them. The adoration takes. Someone like Henry gets fed on that, and slowly, maybe, he begins to crawl out."

The "success" stories define success as a moment-to-moment event. The reason that the Center itself has been successful on its own terms is that it both expects the impossible and does not expect too much. Whole-cloth conversions of life habits and of character are not the Sisters' goals. A small improvement is a great event; a single flash of self-awareness in a client, a revelation. The Center will not give up on Henry's mother any more than it would give up on Henry, but it expects no miracles. Things go forward and things go back; that is taken for granted. The Center, too, operates *in via*. Its diverse efforts on behalf of family life function like a constant sound in Sunset Park, an unwavering voice that continues to deliver its rational message equally on quiet Sunday afternoons and on nights of mayhem.

"You wonder why the staff does this work," Mary Paul told me once. "People who are in what we call the helping professions are curious. I think they may feel something missing in their lives. There can be a lot of ego in this profession, a lot of vicarious fulfillment. One wants to see oneself as a good and giving person. There is nothing wrong with that, but it can't be the only goal. The ultimate goal must be a change in the system in which both the giver and the taker live. Life is made better generally. I bet if you had time to interview every one of our clients, many would not attribute changes that occurred to us at all. Good things happened, and they believe they were their achievements. In many ways they were.

"People call us a charity organization. I don't like the word charity, except in the sense of caritas, love. Love is not based on marking people up by their assets and virtues. Love is based on the sense of the mystery of the person. The gratitude I feel is that I am able to see this particular person at this particular time. Yet the person remains an unfathomable mystery and is going somewhere I will never know."

Sixteen teenagers in a circle run in place, snap their fingers, clap their hands under their legs as they lift them. Much giggling and groaning. Jokes about Jane Fonda. Stretch exercises on the cafeteria floor of P.S. 1. Julie Stein Brockway wears a sweatshirt reading NAGS HEAD, NORTH CAROLINA. Calls out directions: "Let's do knots." Kids divide into two huddles, all crossing arms, grasping one another. Entangled, they must work their way out by twisting until their knot unravels. "Anita's stuck again." Laughter. Julie: "Double duck-ducks, please." Kids on haunches in one large circle again. Hector, tagged "Goose," has to run outside the circle to tag Felice. Slips and collisions. Howls, exaggerated pain. Circle re-forms. Julie: "Huggy-bear two." Kids embrace in pairs. "Huggy-bear five." Kids embrace in clusters of five. Hector to me: "Love at first sight." This is an elimination game. Last boy pretends to weep with self-pity, moans, "Rejected." Julie again: "Emotional machines." Kids make instant clusters, constructs of their bodies. In a cluster one girl cries; another spanks her; a boy rocks on the floor as he clings to the second girl's leg; another boy pulls that boy's foot. "Too easy," Julie shouts. "Take your risks, ladies and gentlemen. Family machines." A girl begins, "Gimme," and continues repeating the word as the start of a roundelay. A boy chips in "No," and continues to say "No." Second boy: "It's mine." Second girl: "Will you stop whining?" Third boy: "Shut up." The family machine roars. Applause, whistles, whoops. Circle again. Julie: "Start a feeling." One: "I'm happy." Each follows with own intonation until "I'm happy" goes round once. Another: "I'm so frustrated." Another: "Why do you do this to me?" Julie: "Carlos, don't say it until you feel it." Another feeling starts: "I'm so cool." Another: "I've got chirasma." The whole group: "What?" Boy, confused, repeats, "I've got chirasma." Girl: "You mean you got asthma." Laughter. "You mean you got charisma." Julie: "Let's do it. Keep moving. Today we've got chirasma."

The Center for Family Life is a model of a community-based program in a poor urban neighborhood, yet the problems of American families are hardly limited to poverty or to cities. The fact that Henry is poor and black, and that he lives in violent circumstances, makes him an unusually dramatic and sadly familiar example of mistreatment. For what he represents, however, he could be any child anywhere in the country.

I could have the wrong Henry. Henry is not a poor, black sixteen-year-old from Sunset Park, Brooklyn. He is a rich, white sixteen-year-old senior at the Groton boarding school, who has just cheated on his Greek exam, because his father, a true-blue Yalie, yells at him constantly for being stupid and retarded, and for not being good enough to get into Yale. No, I am wrong again. That isn't Henry, either. Henry is a twelve-year-old girl from Corpus

Christi, Texas, who is trying to get pregnant "to have love in my life." Or is that a different Henry? Maybe the Henry I am thinking of is the six-year-old girl who was beaten to death by her adoptive parents in a brownstone in Greenwich Village some years ago. Or the Henry whose father set him on fire to strike back at his wife in a custody case? Or is Henry those teenagers who made a suicide pact in New Jersey? I have it. Henry is the toddler in Los Angeles, whose mother squeezed him between a table and a sofa for punishment, and whose last words were "Me no breathe."

Here's Henry now. That's his key in the door. His folks are both at work, and will be out till midnight. He has the house to himself. He pours himself a Coors, calls his girl to come over, and plunks down in front of the TV to watch the Jenny Jones Show bring him a picture of America.

In fact, the Henry of Sunset Park is considerably luckier than the tens of millions of American children, of all economic classes, races, and regions, whom the country pretends to love. At least this Henry has an effective local social service agency in the Center that is devoted to his well-being.

In 1994, an estimated 2,936,000 children were reported to public social service agencies for abuse and/or neglect by adults. Approximately 1,111 of these died that year as a result of abuse and/or neglect. At the end of FY 1994, it was estimated that nationwide, 466,000 children were in foster care or some similar substitute homes. This represents a 65 percent increase since 1986. In 1994, 14.0 million children under the age of eighteen were living in poverty, an estimated 10,000 of whom died as a direct result of their poverty. Approximately 100,000 children are homeless. The American Humane Association reports that since 1988, American teenage boys are more likely to die from gunshot wounds than from all other natural causes combined. Two studies of teenage pregnancy, from Seattle and Chicago, state that approximately 65 percent of teenage mothers reported being sexually abused at one point in their lives.

Such figures are fairly well known, though that has not improved any of the situations. Less familiar are the figures indicating where America stands in its treatment of children in relation to other countries, both the highly industrialized countries and those of the Third World. In 1991, America ranked thirty-first in percentage of low-birthweight babies, behind such countries as Turkey, Romania, and Iran. It ranked seventeenth in the world in immunizations against polio, behind Mexico, Albania, and Pakistan. In 1990, America ranked twentieth in infant mortality rates. Sixty-seven newborns die every day in the United States. In Japan the number is thirty-seven. A 1990 report of the Select Committee on Children, Youth and Families that compared American children with those of other advanced industrialized countries found that the U.S. (and Australia) had the highest percentage of children in poverty (15 percent).

In education, most international surveys show that American children rank seventh out of ten countries in physics; ninth out of ten in chemistry; and tenth out of ten in math. In a study by the International Association of Educational Achievement, American ninth graders tied for fourteenth place in science with Singapore and Thailand. Ninety percent of Japanese children complete high school, compared with 73 percent of Americans. These figures may have something to do with the fact that the House of Representatives Appropriations Committee recently voted to reduce education funding by $3.9 billion, or 15.9 percent. One might expect defense to be cut by much less (0.3 percent). But agriculture is being reduced by only 9 percent, and transportation by 7 percent.

While it is true that poor children, black and white, suffer a disproportionate share of ills, the increasing destruction of the American young occurs in the rural regions, as well as in the cities, and among the middle class and upper classes, too. Responses to a survey of girls in grades 6 to 12 in mainly Midwestern states, in 111 communities with populations under 100,000, indicated that by grade nine, one in five girls had been sexually abused. By grade ten, the number was one in five; and one in three girls had been abused physically, sexually, or both. The survey defined physical abuse as an adult causing a scar, bruises, welts, bleeding, or a broken bone, and sexual abuse as a family member or "someone else" imposing sexual behavior on the child. In 1993, there were 19,466 reports of child abuse involving 30,000 children made to the Iowa Department of Human Services. Girls, Inc. in Omaha states that sexual abuse of girls reported in Nebraska (three in a class of twenty-five) is that of the national average.

Statistics on the poor are more available than those on better-off families because better-off families are able to insulate themselves, and to hide; welfare agencies rarely invade the homes of the rich.

But the mistreatment of American children is a middle-class problem. Russell Johnson, director of the Human Services Department in Cleveland, Ohio's Medina County, estimates that up to 40 percent of abused children in the county come from middle-class or upper-income households. A random sampling of adolescents in Minnesota found that 6 percent of middle- or middle-to-high-income families had at least one child in alcohol or drug treatment programs by ages 14 to 17. Adolescents in an additional 5 percent of families were using as much alcohol and drugs as the kids who were in treatment. Middle-class whites like to think that kids with guns is a black or Latino inner-city menace exclusively. But William C. Haynes, of the Juvenile Justice Department in Memphis, reports that groups of rich white kids with guns opened fire on each other recently. There have been drive-by shootings in Des Moines, Iowa. Richard Louv, the author of *Childhood's Future*, notes that the shooting programs of the 4H clubs drew at least 100,000 kids at the end of the 1980s, a tenfold increase since the mid-1980s.

Two middle-class parents who work full-time will naturally spend less time with their children. In 1976, according to economist Sylvia Hewlett, author of *When the Bough Breaks*, 11 percent of children under the age of one year had mothers in the work force. By 1988, the number had risen to 51 percent. Another economist, Victor Fuchs, contends that children have lost 10 to 12 hours a week of parental time since 1960, due to the added number of hours that both parents work. A Louis Harris poll states that the average work week rose to 52.2 hours; small business people, an average of 57.3 hours. At an art exhibit of children's paintings at Christie's in New York City last year, paintings were displayed depicting "Images of Mothers and Fathers." One, showing a man with his hands held up in surrender, and who was surrounded by clocks, carried the caption: "This is my father." A ninth-grader drew a picture of her mother as a clock.

Violent and destructive behavior by middle- and upper-middle-class kids is a daily news story. A couple of years ago, in the placid seaport town of Dartmouth, Massachusetts, three teenagers burst into a high school classroom, beat a freshman over the head with a baseball bat, and stabbed him in the abdomen to death. Recently, in the same sort of town in Tennessee, a boy driving the new car that his parents had just bought him, shot and killed a horse in a field, for the fun of it. High school kids go on destructive binges in Billings, Montana. In 1989, ABC's television newsmagazine, "20/20" ran a piece on high-living teenagers in wealthy Pacific Palisades, California, who were lost to drugs and drink. NBC news showed a video of middle-class teenagers in Florida, on a rampage. They tore apart elegant homes and cooked family pets in the microwave. The teenagers shot the video themselves.

Divorce is not always a destructive event in a child's life, but it is more often so than the divorcing parents care to admit. Half the number of all divorced fathers do not see their children after the break-up, and two-thirds fail to pay child support. One father explained that he could not pay child support because he needed the money to board his two Doberman pinschers. Even when both parents maintain contact with the children, the children can pay. The headmaster of one of New York's distinguished private schools tells me of an afternoon when he was summoned to the school lobby where two parents were shouting and fighting. Each had thought that that weekend was the one in which he or she was to take their child. When the headmaster arrived on the scene, the parents were yanking at the child's arms, stretching him between them.

If some wealthier parents are not looking out for their children, they are looking out for themselves. Many young couples simply do not have children even if they are able to, because a child will cut into their income and into their time for self-interested pursuits. In *Habits of the Heart*, Robert Bellah pointed out that since 1965, Americans have been hooked on the "therapeutic mentality." Christopher Lasch concluded that therapy has replaced religion in American adult lives. A guidance counselor in Alabama tells me one reason that many parents of the children with whom she deals do not come home at night: they are taking therapy classes to help them be better parents.

In the 1850s the Reverend Samuel Arnold of Ossippee, New Hampshire, nearly beat his adopted son to death, because the boy failed to pronounce the words *utter* and *gutter* to the reverend's satisfaction. One day in 1985, a man in Sunset Park wanted to show off how smart his six-year-old son was, and forced him to read from a book in front of me. When the boy mispronounced the word *bite* as *bit*, his father slammed his fist on the kitchen table and made him reread the story from the beginning.

Individual parents may love their kids, but the society seems to wish the children dead. It is as if children are seen as interfering with life, rather than perpetuating it. Modern living is too difficult, too much to handle or to bear. Children get in the way of one's pleasure or of one's survival. Worse, like Henry, they remind adults of their incapacity to love them.

Jennifer Zanger says: "We spend so much time protecting ourselves from the realities because we can't bear to see what we are doing to our kids. How could we live with ourselves if we really knew what we are creating?"

She started working with Henry after the incident involving his mother's boyfriend. She had seen him around the Center but had no idea of the trouble in his life until he approached her the day he testified against the boyfriend in court. His mother was shutting him out. "'I need to talk to you,' he told me. Then he burst into tears.

"The situation was terrible in the beginning. His mother did not speak to him for three whole months. The afternoon that Geraldine and I first went over to their house, the mother pulled a kitchen knife on Henry. He stood there helplessly, repeating, 'I don't want to hurt you.' And she kept screaming at him.

"But now we meet regularly with her and with them both. She is beginning to come around. Often what it takes is to make people see clearly what they're doing to someone else. Once that happens, a family begins to regroup.

"Henry has a very tender heart. He is struggling with the question of whether it is possible to feel something without being hurt. Once he came to me and said: 'I saw something in the park today that almost made me tear. A mother and her daughter were sitting on a bench. The mother said, 'I love you.' And the daughter said, 'I love you.' I thought: Can people really be that way? And then I thought: 'Nah.'

"He is very gentle. He's wonderful with little kids in the summer camp. He would never harm a smaller child. But if an older person attacks or offends him, he is livid beyond control. He is so deeply hurt that the slightest thing sets him off. Fighting is a power issue for him. He tells me, 'When I'm in a fight, I think of my mother and it gives me the energy.'

"This graffiti business, this 'writing up.' I've said to him so many times: 'Please. Explain it to me. I want to understand.'

Because he keeps getting arrested for these petty offenses, and they're building up to a point where a prosecutor will want to put him away. One time he was arrested for writing up two days in a row. I get a call and I got down to the 68th Precinct, and there he is, no shoes on, handcuffed to the bench. The cop was awful. She said: 'I hope you go to jail because that's where you deserve to be.' So I wind up being on Henry's side, even though I want to confront him for doing the wrong thing.

"And the third day, there is Henry again, down at the station house, handcuffed to the bench. I said to him: 'Look. If you want to spend time with me, just say so. We'll go do something. You don't need to get arrested to get my attention.' He said, in that glum way of his, 'Very funny, Jennifer.' But on the way out, he leans down and tells me: 'You shouldn't help me. You should help someone else. It's past my time already.' He was fifteen."

Sitting with Henry in the P.S. 314 classroom, I ask him what he thinks about when he's alone.

"I think about the future, about getting out of here. I'd like to live somewhere else, upstate maybe. I wouldn't want to grow up and have a kid and live in this neighborhood. It's too dangerous.

"That man who held a gun to my head 'cause he wanted my fronts? I told him: 'I won't take 'em off for you or anybody.'"

"Why not give him the fronts?" I ask.

"It's the way I am."

"Did you think he would shoot you?" He shrugs.

I ask him: "How would you treat a kid of your own?"

"I wouldn't hit him. I'd never hit him. If you hit a kid, he cries at first. Then he stops crying after a while and he doesn't care. You can hit him forever and it won't matter."

"Have people hit you?" He nods. "What for?"

"Writing up."

"Why do you keep doing it?"

"I don't know," he says. "I know it gets me into trouble, but I just can't stop."

"What do you write?"

"TM1," he says. "Everywhere I see some open space I write it. TM1. In the hallways, on the buildings, I just have to see it."

"What does TM1 mean?"

He looks me in the eye for the first time. "The Magnificent One," he says.

HOW WE CAN HELP FAMILIES AND THEIR CHILDREN SUCCEED

STEPHEN SHAMES

I have wandered the nether world of poverty for the past thirty years. In 1991, Aperture and the Children's Defense Fund copublished a book of my photos called *Outside the Dream: Child Poverty in America* which showed a world of neglect and despair, punctuated by a few heroes who prospered despite adversity. *Outside the Dream* documents the problem but sheds little light on solutions. After seeing the photos people would remark to me with resignation, "I know poor children are suffering, but what can we do about it?" That tormented me. I wondered why some poor children turned out fine while others failed so miserably. I wondered if there was anything we could do as individuals, as neighbors, and as a nation to help them succeed.

During three decades taking photos for stories on the down and out, on gangs and drugs, child prostitution, kids in jail, homelessness, and family violence, I saw many children fail. But I also saw many resilient children turn out fine so I knew poverty does not insure failure, rather it acts like a trade wind—blowing children off course. Sometimes they get back on track, most often they don't. I started this project to answer the question, What helps children and families succeed? The answers I found are applicable not only to families in urban ghettos and rural slums, but everywhere families are under financial, emotional, or spiritual stress—in short, everywhere.

In 1992, I talked to Bob Curvin and Janice Molnar of the Ford Foundation about doing a book about solutions. They liked the idea. After a year and a half of discussions I received grants from the Ford and the Charles Stewart Mott Foundations. The first thing my program officers, Janice Molnar and Jon Blyth, insisted on was research. With help from national experts (fifteen of whom became the project's advisory committee) and from the Family Resource Coalition (a national membership, consulting, and advocacy organization for family support), veteran researcher Phyllis Stoffman and I read piles of documents and examined more than one hundred programs over a six-month period, visiting some, talking on the phone to others. We compiled a list of places for me to visit and photograph. I was now ready to ride off, camera in hand.

For two years, between September 1994 and October 1996, I traversed this country from Maine to Hawaii, photographing and talking to families who were participating in exceptional yet diverse

Zach Harris, a mentor from Friends of the Children in Portland, Oregon, went to pick up his young friend Shawn to play basketball, but Shawn hadn't done his homework. So through the closed door, Zach tells Shawn that he must stay home and take care of his responsibilities. Friends of the Children is profiled in depth beginning on page 118.

Girls dance at an all-school sing-along during Community Day, hosted by Early Education Services in Brattleboro, Vermont.

neighborhood programs in fifteen states and the District of Columbia. I saw parents who were learning the skills they needed to be more responsible parents and to get better jobs, folks who were helping their local schools, and adults who dedicated their lives to being role models for children and young adults.

Documentation started on Thursday, September 1, 1994, with a meeting at the Family Resource Coalition in downtown Chicago. That same day in another part of the Windy City, an eleven-year-old boy, Robert "Yummy" Sandier, was found dead in a dark walkway. Police believe he was executed by his own gang, after he became the prime suspect in the execution-murder of a fourteen-year-old. Yummy made the cover of *Time* magazine, his life and death a symbol of the failure of the child welfare system. What can be done? My final day of photography, exactly two years, twenty-eight days and eighty thousand miles later, provided an answer. Watching my new friends Luz and Irma take their wedding vows in front of their family, friends, and their children, I thought about all they had overcome just to be there. I recalled how Avance's parenting program had helped them every step of the way. Then Yummy entered my thoughts. Maybe if his mom had joined a program like Avance, he and the boy he killed would be alive today. I was moved as I reflected on the miracles I had witnessed during an incredible two-year odyssey of change and hope. I learned that we can change how children turn out. I have seen it with my own eyes.

At times the journey was confusing, at times, overwhelming. I didn't know how to make sense of what I was seeing. About halfway through I had a dream, a defining vision. That day I had been in a summer school classroom with ten-year-old T.R. When I first met him eighteen months earlier, he wore a gold chain, an earring, and an "attitude" that caused him to be regularly suspended from school. Zach Harris, a mentor from Friends of the Children in Portland, Oregon, started working with him. Now, a year and a half later, I watched this young man with the hair-trigger temper calmly help another boy learn to read. As the other kid became frustrated, T.R. gently urged him, "Now relax, shut your eyes. Take a break. Then when you're ready we'll try again. You can do it." I almost fell off my chair. Was this the same kid? Was it possible he could change so much, so fast? That night I dreamed I saw the "Hands of God" (similar to the Michelangelo fresco in the Sistine Chapel) reaching down through Zach, touching T.R. With his intense caring, Zach was literally changing the child he was mentoring. I realized the solution to our woes is what good parents have done for generations—provided their children with love, wisdom, and guidance, taught them values and offered a safe haven from a stormy and uncertain world. Community-based programs across America are doing the same thing: transmitting love to parents and children through the hands of caring adults.

The black-and-white photographs in this book show how—right now, as you read this—neighborhood programs are helping families and children succeed in communities across America. Some have been doing it for a quarter century. What they do does not involve space age technology. The home-grown solutions documented in this book are also the answer to how we reverse some of the alarming trends—teenage pregnancy and out-of-wedlock births, crime and violence, welfare and unemployment—that threaten to overwhelm our great nation.

I have seen it. You will see the results with your eyes, too. The programs I photographed are presented in a photo essay of seven sections. Four of these sections are in-depth profiles of specific parenting, mentoring, and family support programs. The other three sections contain programs united by common goals—economic development, community involvement in schools, and youth development.

These programs showed me that we know how to raise successful children because we know what children need. Emotionally, children need love, values, discipline, and a feeling of safety and security (which includes not only protection from abuse and violence but also protection from chaos). Children need to see justice and order in their lives and in the larger world. Intellectually, young people need an education that provides them with reading, math, computer skills and prepares them to think creatively and to solve problems. Physically, kids need food, clothing, shelter, and medical care. Most importantly, all children need intense, positive relationships with caring adults.

But even though we know what kids need, we don't always give it to them. Raising children is hard work. Raising our son Josh took a lot of effort by his mom and me. Josh just graduated from college and we are proud of him, but it didn't just happen. It took time, effort, and money. And it required knowledge and skills in addition to our love. Knowing how to be a good parent is not something anyone is born with. Phyllis and I had to learn how to be good parents as we went along. We learned from family members, friends, neighbors, and professionals such as doctors, nurses, teachers, and clergy.

We all need the knowledge and support of others. Needing help is a natural part of life, asking for help is a sign of strength—not weakness. We sometimes forget nuclear families cannot do it alone. They never have. For families under stress—and families living in poverty definitely are—the challenges of meeting children's needs are even greater. That is where the community-based programs in this book come in. Acting as a combination of family, neighbor, and professional, they help parents meet their children's needs.

All the programs in this book believe that the vast majority of parents love their children and want them to succeed. No parent says of a newborn, "I want Joey to grow up to be a criminal and wouldn't little Alice make a great hooker." The problem is not one of motivation but skills. Most parents are doing the best job they can. But some parents lack the knowledge and resources they need to reach their goals. When I talk to parents about their dreams for their children, they usually mention college and jobs. But when I ask them, "How do you intend to get there?" I sometimes draw blank looks. They have no idea.

Some of these programs help people change their whole frame of reference and their strategies for navigating through life. Change is hard work. Last year I sat next to a woman on an airplane who

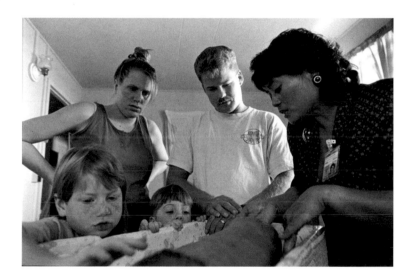

The U.S. Armed Forces believe that the best way to reduce child abuse and domestic violence is to prevent it by teaching military moms and dads how to be better parents. In Hawaii, the military sponsors ASPECTS, a program that offers prospective parents information about prenatal care, childbirth, parenting, and infant care.

Kathy English, Director of Community Health Nursing for ASPECTS, says, "The military is big on parenting for young children. It is a readiness issue. If soldiers are having a problem at home they are not going to do as well in the field. How well are they going to function in their unit in Haiti if they are worrying about the wife they left behind? So we work to strengthen the whole family."

Below: The Institute for Responsible Fatherhood and Family Revitalization encourages young men to legally establish paternity, to get jobs and support their families, and to become involved in the lives of their children in a loving, compassionate, and nurturing way. The Center also works with couples to improve their relationships. Charles Ballard, founder of the program, believes that this relationship is primary; and if it is functioning well, the parents will be able to successfully nurture their children.

Opposite left: At the Kelly Elementary School's Parent Center in Portland, Oregon, children and their parents tell "family stories." A ball of yarn is passed from one storyteller to the next to illustrate that everyone is bound to others.

Opposite right: Through Early Education Services in Brattleboro, Vermont, paraprofessional home educators visit parents and their preschool children at home, bringing activities that help prepare the little ones to start school.

changes corporate cultures for a living. She told me it takes a total commitment from top management, clear goals, millions of dollars, and three to five years to change a corporate culture. We are talking about changing the culture of people who can be fired if they don't go along with the program. Why are we surprised that social programs don't achieve instant success? We make no long-term commitment to them. We set conflicting goals. We give them minimal appropriations and not enough staff. Then we expect them to work miracles in a few months. This is not realistic.

We know that changing behavior takes time and a coordinated effort. If we want children to succeed we must start early, then keep on going. Houses need good foundations. So do children. That is why we must start at birth. All the literature on early childhood tells us the first three years of a child's life are the most important. During the first three years—long before children get to school—they are taught to succeed or fail by their first teachers, their parents. That is why the best way to help children is to help their parents do their job.

Recently Ron Kotulak, a journalist who received a Pulitzer Prize for his reporting on the brain, wrote in his marvelous book *Inside the Brain: Revolutionary Discoveries of How the Mind Works,* "I always thought you were born with a brain and that's it. Now we know it's the environment that is crucial in establishing the kind of brain the child is going to have. . . . Genes establish the framework of the brain, but the external environment provides the customized finishing touches. . . . It is critical to get in and insure proper stimulation to build a good brain." Dr. Daniel Alkon, chief of the Neural Systems Laboratory at the National Institutes of Health, explains in a July 23, 1996, article in the *New York Times,* "DNA does not contain enough information to specify how the brain finally gets wired. The newborn brain comes equipped with a set of genetically based rules for how learning takes place and is then literally shaped by experience." "Early experiences are so powerful," according to pediatric neurobiologist Harry Chungai of Wayne State University (quoted in *Newsweek* on February 19, 1996), "they can completely change the way a person turns out."

While genetics do not predetermine everything, neither is the brain a blank slate. Torsen Wiesel and David Hubel of Harvard Medical School received a Nobel Prize for illustrating that the brain has windows of opportunity that are open for short periods, especially during the first three years. Even though learning can take place throughout life, if you miss the window you're playing with a

handicap. For example, capacity for math and logic develops by age four; language by age ten. Children learn how to handle their emotions, how they will relate to others, and whether they can trust the world to be a safe place by age two, a period in our lives when we will have few conscious memories. It is critical to insure proper stimulation—talking to a baby, showing her pictures, reading books to him—because a parent's touch literally shapes a baby's brain development. Researchers have demonstrated that a stimulating environment can boost a kindergartner's IQ score by up to fifteen points.

The brain develops better when exposed to positive stimulation and love. It is adversely affected by a hostile environment. Ron Kotulak writes, "Neglect (the lack of proper stimulation) and abuse (overexposure to the wrong kind of stimulation) are two sides of the same coin. Both change the brain's development adversely and permanently. . . . One of the more astounding discoveries is that stresses caused by bad experiences can actually affect genes, switching them on or off at the wrong times. Environmental stress can activate genes linked to depression and other mental problems. Environmentally induced brain changes can become permanent in an individual, encoding into genes a propensity for aggression and violence that can last a lifetime."

This doesn't mean that we should just give up on people who have had bad childhoods. I know that this is true. I am one of these people. Because of my horrendous childhood, I have to climb out of a deep hole every morning. Yet I *am* able to cope and I was able to raise my son differently from the way my parents raised me. That is because there are other factors such as resiliency, later posi-

tive experiences, and desire to change that help people overcome early damaging experiences. In my life, an ninth grade teacher, my wife, and her father helped me see that life could be better.

So even though mentoring and other later experiences can change people's lives, we shouldn't underestimate the importance of early childhood. One way to think about this is by analogy to physical health. We know that proper diet and exercise help reduce heart attacks. Of course we still treat people when they have heart attacks. It isn't an either/or choice. However, if we want to remain healthy, we need to emphasize prevention since hardened arteries are difficult to reverse and open heart surgery is expensive.

Similarly, the best way to reduce teenage pregnancy and family violence and to insure that all children reach their full potential is to create loving, enriching environments for infants and toddlers. Strong families protect children. According to the Carnegie Foundation's report "Starting Points," "Research indicates the strongest buffer for young children is a supportive relationship with parents. Most children are able to adjust to living in dangerous situations as long as their parents are not stressed beyond their capacity to cope."

Since mom and dad are the most important people in a child's life and the parent-child relationship is the most important factor in a child's success, we need to do everything we can to help parents do their jobs better. The family support programs in this book do that. They help parents create a road map for reaching their goals and teach them the skills necessary to make the journey. They inform parents about child development and parenting strategies. They emphasize the importance of literacy and education. They reinforce basic moral values. Neighborhood family

Robert Moses, legendary civil rights organizer and founder of the Algebra Project, views algebra as "the gateway" to full participation in society—as important to citizenship as was the vote in the 1960s. The Algebra Project uses a hands-on method to teach children math.

resource centers are places where parents talk to each other, cement friendships, and build support networks. These programs also help parents further their education and get better jobs.

Georgette Chapas, a home visitor who graduated from the parent education program at Avance, told me, "I found new ideas about how to discipline my son. I learned it is better to guide him, it is better to communicate with him rather than hit him. When I got upset I used to hit him. I was spanking him all the time. If he spilled the soda, I'd respond with the negative. In Avance, I learned to be more patient, to teach him how to solve the problem, to help him learn to wipe up his spill rather than spank him and yell at him. In Avance they explain to you why this is important. They tell you why children have accidents. How can we expect them to be perfect when we make mistakes ourselves?

"One thing I teach parents [in home visits] is to be positive. Children need praise. I encourage parents to have a lot of eye contact with their children, to talk to them at their level. I tell them to treat their kids the same way they want to be treated. Teaching manners is another way to teach respect for others." Parents learn problem-solving skills from neighbors like Georgette Chapas. They also learn that poverty is not a hindrance to teaching their children everything they need to know to succeed in America.

Helping parents is the best way to help children. First of all, we have no choice but to rely on parents, especially in these budget-conscious times. Secondly, governments don't raise kids well. So while some kids must not be allowed to live with their parents, relying on orphanages or foster care to parent large numbers of children will bankrupt us. Good institutional care costs about $30,000 annually per child, much more than it costs a parent to raise a child. Isn't it better to invest the money and energy to help parents?

We have to start with early childhood programs that support parents of little kids, but we can't stop there. We must keep going.

We need to continue giving children and youth attention for the same reason we don't ignore our own children when they turn five. People need stuff all their lives. My dad is dying as I write this. Although I am fifty, I still need him. So why shouldn't a seven-year-old or a teenager need an adult's help? Young people need adults to guide them. Good parents do things for kids not only to avoid problems but because those things are good for kids. I didn't send my son to camp or involve him in sports merely to keep him out of trouble. His mom and I wanted Josh to have fun and grow as a person. We wanted to build his character. We need to keep youths occupied with positive activities like art, music, dance, sports, and community service so they can gain knowledge, learn respect, experience success, and learn to be part of a team. Youth groups do this and so much more. Perhaps the most important thing youth organizations do is let young people hang out with their dedicated staff. Intense, positive relationships are especially important to adolescents who are breaking away from their parents and need someone to show them the skills and responsibilities that go with their new adult bodies. This period of rapid physical growth, increased brain activity, and psychological turmoil is almost as important as early childhood. It is a time when young people can veer terribly off track, fall into gangs, experiment with sex or drugs. Who they latch onto, whether a teacher or a drug dealer, determines what kind of adult they grow into.

All teenagers need mentors, even if they have great parents. But this may be the only chance for kids in troubled families. The reality is that not all parents are positive role models for their kids. We can't write off all kids who have "bad" parents and just build jail cells for them. Not only is this cruel and expensive, it doesn't achieve our goals. It does not create public safety. When successful adults are asked what one factor made a difference in their lives, most say an intense, positive relationship with an adult when they were young.

In Albert Camus's autobiographical novel, *The First Man*, he tells a story about a poor, fatherless boy and two of his friends who had their lives turned around by their teacher. "They felt for the first time that they existed and that they were the objects of the highest regard: they were judged worthy to discover the world." Camus relates how this teacher nominated him for a secondary school scholarship, talked his grandmother into letting him attend, and prepared him for the exam. Without this teacher the world might have lost one of its great writers. How many other talented poor children need mentors, but don't have them? Perhaps the one who will discover the cure for cancer.

Whether aimed at creating jobs, educating parents, or mentoring teens; whether started by conservatives or liberals, by people who pray every day or those who haven't seen the inside of a church in decades, by schoolteachers or businessmen; whether staffed by men or women, African-Americans, Asians, Pacific Islanders, Hispanics, Native Americans, or Caucasians, all the programs in this book teach living skills in a framework that emphasizes personal responsibility and values. And they all have the following seven characteristics:

1. They are locally run and participation is voluntary. Community programs are accepted because they are part of the neighborhood, not bureaucratic, patronizing or condescending. Staff often live in the neighborhood. These organizations hire and train neighborhood people for jobs as paraprofessionals. Sometimes it is their first "white collar" job experience, a stepping stone to a better career or a college degree.

A major advantage of hiring community members is that they understand the area and its needs. Many went through the programs themselves. They can say, "I was like you. I did it, you can, too." People think of them as neighbors because they are. Their kids attend the same schools and pray in the same churches, synagogues, and mosques as program participants.

Further, the programs are voluntary. People have to want help. And they do. I have witnessed this all over America. If we spend the next twenty years helping only those who want to improve their lives, we would still have a long waiting list. There are plenty of people out there who need and want our help, resources, and support.

2. Program staff and participants form intense, caring relationships. Staff treat people respectfully and as partners. That is why

The FACE Program operates a parenting center on an isolated Navajo reservation in Torreon, New Mexico, and provides home visits to families with young children, offering family literacy instruction, parenting information, and referrals to other services.

Avance Family Support and Education Program in Texas encourages parents to take an active in interest in children's "work"—including helping their kids with homework. Avance is profiled in depth beginning on page 42.

they are often considered extended family members. These positive relationships are the basis for everything that goes on in community-based programs.

3. Staff teach responsibility by living it. The "ordinary heroes" who run community programs put their values into practice. Nobody likes being lectured to, young people especially; they learn by seeing. If I instruct my son on honesty and then walk out of a restaurant without paying, what will he learn—what I said or what I did? People who work in community programs teach parents to respect their kids by treating moms and dads with fairness and dignity. They assume people have strengths and build on these instead of tearing down people's bad habits. This positive approach works because many of these community workers are exemplary individuals. People follow their examples willingly because they admire them.

Teaching responsibility is the core of any community program. Since the family plays the main role in the moral life of children, programs support the moral choices families make. Programs encourage education and the work ethic. Not surprisingly, family centers often work closely with local religious institutions. (In fact, one third of the programs in this book were started by church-affiliated people.) The message of responsibility improves relationships between husband and wife, parents and children.

4. Programs strengthen what is good in their community. Families cannot provide a moral environment all by themselves, especially if the neighborhood fights their efforts. It is hard to make good choices if all a child sees out his window is bad. Programs are not islands. They are catalysts connecting people to other individuals and institutions in their community, such as schools.

It is impossible to think of helping children and ignore schools. Virtually every organization included in this book is involved with the area school. Residents and staff teach classes, help teachers in the classroom, provide after-school care, run summer programs, mentor students, run workshops for parents, provide social services in schools, make sure students get to school safely, sit on school governing boards.

The essence of community organizations is bringing people together to improve the neighborhood. These collaborations make communities more livable by helping residents make them safer and by coordinating community resources. Groups in this book have coordinated efforts with police, housing authorities, hospitals and medical providers, psychological and family counselors, local, state, and federal government agencies, the business community, volunteer and service organizations, and churches. Neighborhood programs promote economic development, rehabilitate housing, and fight crime.

We all know having more police on the streets reduces crime. I saw this myself in 1992 and 1993 when for five months I rode with the Houston Police Department's Homicide Squad. In addition to locking up serious offenders and closing crack houses, the New York Police Department found that by cracking down on quality of life offenses such as graffiti, public drinking, and loitering, they have been able to make more arrests for gun possession and take violent criminals off the streets. The rate of murder and serious crime has fallen much more there than in the country as a whole. In addition, according to Malcolm Galdwell, reporting in *The New Yorker,* June 3, 1996, "Car thefts have fallen to seventy-one thousand down from a hundred and fifty thousand as recently as six years ago. Burglaries have fallen from more than two hundred thousand in the early nineteen-eighties to seventy-five thousand in 1995." Police in San Diego, New Haven, Philadelphia, and Honolulu use community policing to reduce crime in their cities.

Community organizations also have an important role to play in crime reduction. By providing mentoring and role models to youngsters, by rehabilitating housing, and fixing the broken win-

John Marshall Elementary School in San Diego, California, brings social services into the school to make them more convenient for families to use, and to encourage parents to come to the school and to get involved in their children's education. Since more than two-thirds of John Marshall students are from foreign countries, the school employs ethnic coordinators, who serve as cultural liaisons.

Top: The school's Somali coordinator translates at a parent-teacher conference, so that the mother can understand how her children are doing in school.

dows in their neighborhoods, community organizations are helping reduce crime by stopping it before it gains a foothold.

In 1996, the Rand Corporation published the results of their study on the effectiveness of dollars spent to reduce juvenile and adult crime. They compared California's three strikes law with home visits beginning before birth going up to the age of two; parent training and therapy for families with very young children who "act out" in school; cash and other graduation incentives for high school students; and supervision of high school youths who have exhibited delinquent behavior. They evaluated not only the effectiveness of each in reducing criminal behavior but the effectiveness per dollar spent. (They did not look at the positive effects of home visiting or consider money saved by not having to maintain someone in prison, they only compared the cost of the program and the decrease in the crime rate.)

The Rand study found that three of the interventions studied were comparable to three strikes in reducing crime, at a much lower cost. The report cautions, "None of this suggests that incarceration is the wrong approach. The crime reductions achievable through additional incarceration—on the order of 20 percent or so—are substantial. But with 80 percent of serious crime remaining, Americans will want to know what else can be done. It might be inferred from California's vote in favor of the three strikes law that the public believes a 21 percent reduction in crime is worth the cost of $5.5 billion a year. For less than an additional billion dollars, graduation incentives and parent training could roughly double that crime reduction."

Early home visiting is harder to evaluate since there is "almost a fifteen-year delay between when the intervention is applied and when it begins affecting serious street crimes. . . . However, it affects one form of crime immediately: child abuse by the parents. . . . Recent studies have indicated that about one in ten children are seriously abused or neglected by their parents. The rate is considerably higher among lower socioeconomic groups. The kind of early-childhood intervention considered here has been shown to reduce rates of child abuse by about 50 percent." Not only do abused and neglected children commit a disproportionate share of serious violent crimes when they grow up, but child abuse itself is a crime. So reducing it 50 percent right now should be considered a crime reduction priority. Healthy Start, Hawaii's statewide child abuse prevention program, has proven 99 percent effective at elim-

inating child abuse among participants. It is being replicated in twenty-six states and by the military.

5. Programs create safe havens. Community centers are safe, welcoming places. Responsibility and values start with a safe place. Nothing can happen without safety. This is what parents try to do for their kids. Sometimes they can do it by themselves. But a lot of neighborhoods are not safe. I have spent too many nights on these blocks. I couldn't sleep because of the gunfire. How can kids? I have talked to children who sleep under their beds to avoid stray bullets. I remember a boy in the Bronx saying to me, "If I grow up." Not when I grow up, if I grow up. That is when it really hit me. What kind of values can he have if he isn't even certain he will make it to adulthood? Should he study hard? Should he delay sexual activity? What difference does it make to him if he doesn't think he will make it? Creating a safe place precedes teaching moral choices.

In addition to working with police and others to make the whole neighborhood safer, community programs show people how to cope with not-so-great situations by creating their own safe havens. Many people in poverty are overwhelmed by forces they think are beyond their control, such as poverty, racism, violence, and awful neighborhoods. Programs help people change their internal view of the situation, so they see themselves as able to change and having power to do things about what they experience. Attitude is everything. Community programs help people see opportunities.

6. Programs provide people with opportunities to expand their skills and become economically self-sufficient. Let's face it, you can be the best parent in the world, but if someone in your household doesn't have a decent job, it is next to impossible for your children to succeed. Family support programs help parents develop employment skills. Youth programs link students with part-time jobs. Community development corporations bring businesses to impoverished neighborhoods, train residents for jobs, build or rehabilitate housing, and organize residents block by block to fight crime.

7. Each program has a detailed plan and a strategy for achieving its goals. The work of community programs is to be there for families and children but it is not just hanging around with parents and kids. All of the organizations profiled in this book have a well-articulated philosophy and strategy. They do what they do intentionally, and they change what they do in response to community needs and evaluations of their effectiveness.

These are troubling times. One in four children in America lives in poverty. One in three American children is born to unmarried parents. One in eight is born to a teenage mother. One in four lives with only one parent. One in twenty-five American youths is reported abused or neglected in any year. (That is two million abused children. One-third of these are infants under one year of age.) A child growing up in a poor community plagued by violence is twenty-two times more likely to experience family violence, abuse, or neglect.

Computers make work easier by eliminating repetitive tasks, but they also make possible a global economy that threatens to free many Americans from their jobs. Working families, especially our blue-collar communities, keep our virtues and values alive. As economic times become tougher for average people, family stability is threatened and communities that live our core values are being eroded.

What can we do?

We know what to do, and why it works. Community-based family support organizations, economic development, youth and mentoring programs are giving birth to solutions that are both spiritual and pragmatic. These organizations are vital to our future.

As families become stronger, our nation prospers. Supporting families is going to be even more important during the twenty-first century, as we see greater strains on families. In the 1950s a person could walk from his high school graduation ceremony straight to the factory door and have job security for life. That is no longer possible and there is no reason to believe the economic prospects of middle-class people will improve soon. In the "good old days" communities and extended families helped nurture kids. Today, with both parents working, parents spend 40 percent less time with kids than they did thirty years ago. And relatives are often hundreds of miles away. Community programs can fill the gap. According to Robert Woodson, chairman of the National Center for Neighborhood Enterprise: "Under normal conditions, the natural family is the first and primary source of ethical, moral, and spiritual values. When the family breaks down, what works most effectively is for local people to become an extended, surrogate family."

Community programs form the basis for a coherent family policy. This is the approach our local, state, and federal governments should be taking as we go from welfare to work. This is what corporations and foundations concerned with children and families ought to be funding. The programs in this book offer a range of approaches. If we took the best elements from each of them, we would have the basis for a national policy—not the whole solution but an important part.

While they can do a lot, we must remember that neighborhood programs can't do everything. Economic and trade policies, medical and social security systems cannot be created on a local level. Government still has the obligation to create policy that is supportive of families and communities and to fund efforts that help to mend our fragmented social structure. Local programs cannot "save" everyone nor eliminate poverty; they can help people develop the skills and motivation to surmount the obstacles in

Opposite: The San Diego Police Department's citywide Neighborhood Policing Program reduces crime by developing relationships between neighborhood police officers and residents. Police officers begin by going door-to-door, interviewing residents about their crime-related concerns. They then work with community members to achieve the neighborhood's goals by, among other strategies, organizing neighborhood watches, holding community meetings, educating residents about crime prevention, making arrests, contacting landlords to evict drug dealers, and partnering with other city agencies to improve the quality of life in communities.

Below: Residents of the Bedford-Stuyvesant area of Brooklyn started a volunteer ambulance corps because ambulances did not respond to calls from their dangerous neighborhood. Their first goal was to provide prompt emergency care to residents. Response time is now under two minutes.

Through the Bedford-Stuyvesant Volunteer Ambulance Corps hundreds of neighborhood residents have been trained and certified as Emergency Medical Technicians (EMT) and have used this certification to obtain paying jobs. As part of its youth corps, uniformed teenagers assist EMTs.

O'Farrell Community School for Advanced Academic Studies in San Diego, California, was founded by teachers who believe that every child is capable of doing advanced (college-track) academic work—and half of its students do, compared with 15 percent nationally. The school has a social services wing and runs a number of support groups for kids.

Above: A child draws a picture of her feelings and then discusses them with an adult counselor as part of the Death and Dying Support Group. This group was started to help a number of O'Farrell students who were having trouble in school because they were grieving for loved ones, some of whom were victims of drug overdoses or neighborhood violence.

their lives. People will still have problems. They may remain poor, their high-paying jobs may move thousands of miles away, but they will have the skills and motivation to find alternatives.

Since community organizations are concerned with the rejuvenation of our most important institution, the family, they are an extremely important part of the solution to our nation's problems. If we got together and implemented the time-tested approaches used by these local programs, we would have the basis for a coherent, bipartisan family policy, one that would help children succeed. While funding and running these programs does not guarantee success, not investing in them guarantees failure. Family support can't change the world by itself, but without it all other policies will fail. And the cost of failure is too high. Crime. Teenage pregnancy. Violence. All cost money and all waste lives. If we don't get children off to a good start and keep on going, working with them so they stay on track, we will always be playing catch up, wondering what happened to our teenagers, our once nice neighborhoods, our values. We will ponder forever why the American dream died. Community organizations do what extended families used to do, they preserve our values by helping parents launch their children successfully into the world. That is why neighborhood groups that help families, children, and youth must become the cornerstone of our national policy.

We can do it. Our bipartisan crusade to rid the world of Communism brought the Soviet Union to its knees, but only after we devoted two generations, hundreds of thousands of lives, and trillions of dollars to that effort. It wasn't easy but we had a plan. We hired the best scientists to create sophisticated weapons systems. We experimented. (Many of the weapons systems did not work, but we kept going.) We spent lots of money. (The Soviet Union bankrupted itself trying to compete with us.) We overcame policy differences at least as great as those that divide us today. We didn't give up and we didn't assume it would be quick or stop pursuing our goal because of setbacks and frustrations. We did all this because we saw Communism was a threat to our survival, so we fought it with everything we had. What about the threat of families collapsing? Of children growing up without values? Do we really believe our civilization is at stake? Then we must act.

We need a national commitment. Helping children and families succeed is as important as national defense. It must be our top priority. And when we make the commitment, we must know that, like defeating Communism, helping children won't be easy. But we don't have to reinvent the wheel, we only have to learn from what is happening every day in communities all over America. Why don't we make sure the solutions provided by community organizations are available to every family?

Domestically, we bicker endlessly about family values but don't even support the things that we see have worked in local communities for the past quarter century. We need consensus on goals, a good solid plan, and the fortitude and the money to go forward with that plan. Is there a national leader somewhere in this country who will do for children and families what President Reagan did for the military: give our community programs the support and resources they need to do the job?

We know what to do. We don't need to study this problem. We know we must start early in life. We know good parenting is the key. We know we must support and strengthen families by supporting community values and by teaching skills. We know we must "keep on going" with our kids, keeping them in the web of civilization. We know we must work to improve schools and neighborhoods. We know that neighborhood organizations are the most effective way to build character and increase our moral strength. They inoculate families against failure by encouraging good choices and by helping parents acquire the skills necessary to advance in life. With the help of community-based organizations that provide family support, offer parent education, mentor youth, and encourage community development, we will rebuild the American family and help all of our children succeed. All of us have a responsibility to make this happen by volunteering, by donating money, by supporting policies that are good for families, by being good neighbors. Together we can ensure that America marches into the twenty-first century ready for any challenge because our children will be the best and brightest in the world.

The choice is ours. We know what to do. We just need to do it.

Top: East Bay Center for the Performing Arts in Richmond, California, is a rigorous music, dance, film-making, and theater program that fosters racial harmony and uses the arts as a language to communicate.

Bottom: Manchester Craftsman's Guild (MCG) in Pittsburgh, Pennsylvania uses photography and ceramic arts as ways to engage teens in its youth development program. Mentors work with kids from eleven high schools to encourage them to go on to college. Bill Winston, director of the Guild's Student Development Department, says, "By ninth grade the arrow has already left the bow. If that arrow is not going toward a target that benefits the child, our goal is to bend the trajectory a little bit."

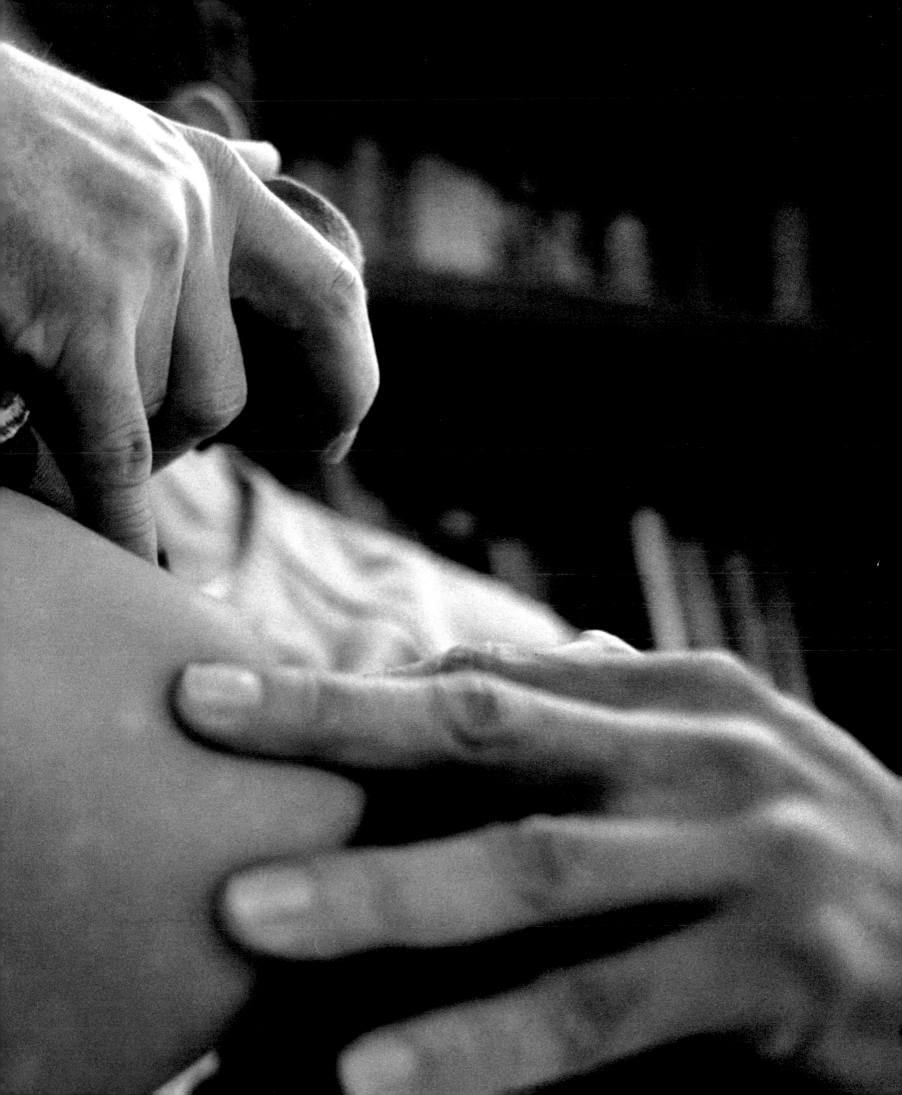

AVANCE FAMILY SUPPORT AND EDUCATION PROGRAM

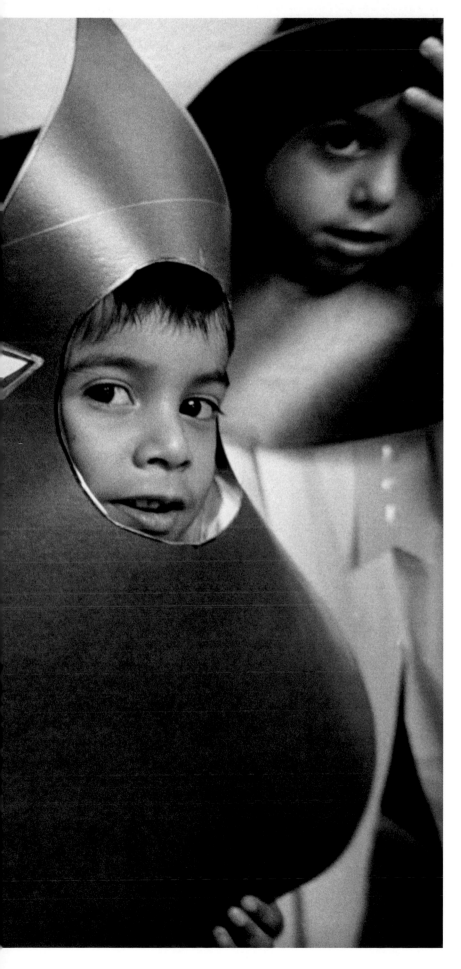

Avance recognizes that parents are the most important people in their children's lives and believes that the best and most cost-effective way to help children succeed is to help their parents. Avance shows parents how to prepare their children for school and for life through its intensive Parent/Child Education Program.

Graduation day is the festive climax of the nine-month program, which consists of weekly three-hour sessions. While children attend a top-notch early childhood education program, parents attend a class on parenting and child development (what they can expect of their children, what methods are likely to be effective with kids at different ages); participate in a toy-making workshop; and hear a presentation by a community member on a topic of interest to parents, such as fire safety or nutrition or cooking.

Class time is also an opportunity for parents to meet neighbors and to develop their support systems. To provide individualized attention, each family is visited at home once a month by an Avance staff member.

In Avance toy-making workshops, parents learn that, even if they don't have much money, they can provide everything their children need to succeed. Expensive, store-bought toys aren't necessary; with a needle and thread, Mom can transform a sock, yarn, and a couple of buttons into a new friend for her three-year-old. With a simple puppet, she can teach her child about colors and textures. "What color are my eyes?" "Where's my nose?" "What color is my hair?" And when her child talks to the puppet, Mom can learn more about what her three-year-old is thinking and feeling.

Gloria Rodriguez, Avance's executive director, says, "After she makes twenty-five or thirty toys, a mother has generalized the concept of teaching, the importance of asking questions, of teaching the colors, the numbers, the shapes and the textures. . . . The beauty of working with the toys is that at the same time as it helps them teach their children, it gives something to the parents. Many of our parents themselves never played as children. So they're sewing and coloring and pasting and cutting and doing all those things that most middle-class children do. They have the freedom to be creative. It makes them take pride."

"I wanted the program to build on the love parents have for their children,"
says Gloria Rodriguez, executive director of Avance.

AVANCE'S STORY

In 1970, Gloria Rodriguez, a first-grade teacher with a master's in early childhood education, was asked by her school principal to "do something" for a group of Hispanic six-year-olds from low-income families that other teachers had labeled "vegetables, slow-learners, and mentally retarded."

She found that the children were not intellectually deficient, but that they did lack what middle-class children typically have: the skills that enable them to start school ready to learn. "They came in with so few experiences in language, in pre-readiness skills like playing and drawing," Rodriguez explains. "I thought that this was because somebody didn't play with them; somebody didn't talk to them; somebody didn't provide the learning environment that's so important in the earlier years."

Rodriguez knew that by the age of four children have learned half of what they're going to learn from birth to age seventeen, and that these early years are not only the time when children develop their language skills, but also when their sense of right and wrong and their basic attitudes toward the world are formed.

Where were these children's parents? Rodriguez talked to them and learned that these parents loved their children very much. They valued education, knew it was the way out of poverty, and wanted their children to succeed in school. "But," Rodriguez says, "They didn't understand their role as the first teachers of their children. They didn't understand what they were supposed to be doing, what skills they needed to be teaching their children." And they had little hope that their children would be able to go farther than they had gone.

Rodriguez thought back to the experiences of families she knew—including her own—who had started out poor and made a better life for their children. "My mother had dreams and aspirations. She kept telling us, 'Life is gonna get better.' But my mother also received support. The support came not only from my grandfather and our extended family, and visiting nurses who came to teach my mother about parenting, but also from neighbors helping neighbors."

Rodriguez dreamed of a center that would offer Latino parents this kind of support and culturally appropriate information about parenting, starting before their child turned three. "I wanted the program to build on the love that parents have for their children," says Rodriguez. "Family is the center of Hispanic culture. . . . 'Respeto' is an important traditional value. I don't care how poor you are, people feel they deserve to be treated with dignity and respect."

That's why, in 1973, she started Avance in San Antonio and began one of the nation's first family support programs. Avance welcomes the entire family and makes special efforts to involve fathers. Rodriguez explains, "In Hispanic culture, you've got to involve the father. Otherwise you're going to break that family. If you have a program that emphasizes family, I don't care how macho the man is, he will allow the woman to go and be a better mother for his children. And he will get involved and find out what he needs to do to keep that family strong."

Over the past twenty-four years, Avance has grown from one small program to more than fifty sites in Texas serving more than 7,000 families each year. It has an annual budget of more than $6 million which is funded by federal, state, and local government as well as private foundations. Programs all over the country use Avance's parenting curriculum and strategies. Evaluations consistently have shown Avance to be successful in meeting its goals. A 1990 longitudinal evaluation found that 90 percent of the children of parents in Avance's first parenting class had graduated from high school; approximately half of those had gone on to college.

But most important is the effect Avance has on families. During and after participating in Avance, parents who have felt overwhelmed, depressed, powerless, and directionless gain control of their lives and consciously embrace their responsibility to be role models and teachers for their children. One parent said, "I've always been a failure, but when I came to Avance, they gave me the courage and strength to believe that I wasn't a failure." The best way to see firsthand the effect of Avance is to get to know participating families. You'll meet such families on the following pages.

Armida Flores, an Avance Parent/
Child Education Program graduate,
now works for Avance as a parenting
instructor. Many families stay involved with Avance after completing
the nine-month parenting program.
The second phase of Avance is formal
education and employment services
for parents. Avance coordinates with
other agencies to offer English as a
Second Language and GED (high

school equivalency) classes and works
with local colleges to enroll parents.
Finally, Avance helps parents get jobs,
both by working with local businesses
and by hiring former participants.

Above: Armida is conducting a home
visit, helping another neighborhood
mother teach numbers to her four-
year-old daughter.

"Children begin learning even before they are born."

When parents enroll in Avance, they fill out a questionnaire; and in response to the question "When do you think your child begins to learn?" most parents answer, "When he starts school." One Avance mother says, "We grew up naïve, not knowing about being parents. So how was I supposed to know how to treat my baby? I would just do what my mom did." Avance teaches parents that children begin learning even before they are born, that the first three years are very important for the future development of a child, and that by making eye contact and talking to their babies they can help them learn and develop.

Many Avance participants are immigrants from Mexico with strong extended family networks, such as the sisters pictured here. Maria and Marixa live next door to each other in an unincorporated rural "colonia," where land is cheap and poor families are able to build their own homes. Maria went through Avance's parenting program, shared what she learned with her sister, and convinced Marixa to enroll.

Susan Martinez, the mother of six children, is twenty-four and has been married for ten years. Her family has been involved with Avance for three years.

SUSAN: Without Avance, I'd never have my GED. They provide the transportation. And they take care of the kids while you go. Before I got into Avance, I wanted to go and get my GED, but I would think, "Well, who's gonna take care of the kids?" Avance gave me this chance.

Susan's husband, Frank, has been in jail twice—once for burglary and again, last year, for a parole violation. He tested positive for marijuana use and spent several months at the county jail. Susan was taking care of her children alone during this time.

FRANK: Well, I guess I was going through my own rough times . . . I guess I was growing up . . . I mean, we started early. But this crisis that I made my family pass though, if it wasn't for Avance, I would have destroyed it. Simply because of my absence. It would have been . . . . I don't know what it would have been.

SUSAN: I think it would have been a disaster, because they helped me and my kids deal with the stress . . .

FRANK: They've been there. They've been there for the family. On our ups. On our downs. I guess you can say we haven't had many ups.

On regular visits to the county jail, Susan and the children talked with Frank through a glass partition. On Saturdays, the children were allowed contact visits.

SUSAN: They have a MATCH/PATCH program (Mothers And Their CHildren/Papas And Their CHildren) inside the jailhouse. And I would take the kids to him every Saturday. It was the bonding routine, the kids and the dad. I didn't want to do that. I didn't want to take them because it was embarrassing. But I couldn't say, "I'm not gonna have the kids go see you." I didn't want them to lose touch with their dad. So I just took them, every Saturday that I could take them.

FRANK: I was, I guess, playing with my family. Like that saying goes, "You don't appreciate something 'til you lose it." Well, I was pretty close to that. I give thanks to God that I didn't lose my family, because I could have. I could have.

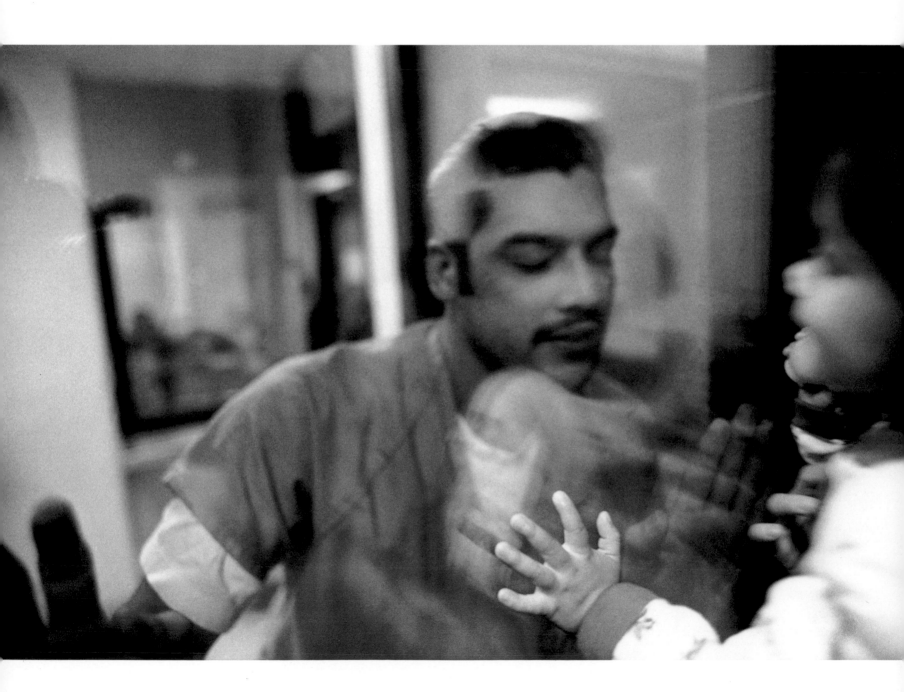

A year later, Frank has a job and is again living with his wife and kids.

FRANK: I'm going to stay out of trouble for my family's sake. Because I can't be playing with their lives anymore. I could ruin them. Like I could have a great impact—a positive impact or I could have a negative impact on them. So I want to just turn my life around. I have to learn to be responsible. To be a dad.

I know that my having been in jail, there's a great percentage that my kids will be there. But I want to break that. I don't have control of the past. If I live today in the present and take one day at a time, I can have impact in the future. I can look back, not to bring myself down, but to say, "Man, where was I? Look where I was. See now I'm not there. I have control of my life." In other words: 'avance' advance, that's what I need to do, advance. Anything to benefit the kids. So we have to improve the parents so the kids will benefit later on down the line. We have to educate . . .

SUSAN: . . . to reach our goal.

Right: Luz and Irma Martinez with their daughter, Pebbles.

LUZ: Growing up, my brothers had long hair: they were all rowdies, they were bad boys. Most of my friends were nothing but bikers, long-hair freaks, tattoos, Harley Davidson, bikini contests, Daisy Dukes, five-band rock, a whole two-week-bike-run. They were dealing in drugs and robbing people, stealing cars, and sometimes I was there and sometimes I wasn't. But it wasn't like I wanted to be like them, I just wanted people to notice me, and I guess, to be honest, she [Irma] is the one who really noticed me and saw through that meanness and that black heart. She brought the real me back out.

IRMA: Yes, he used to go up to the bars and do whatever he wanted to do . . . I said, Your friends get you in trouble and they aren't gonna get you out. I said, That's why you don't need to be hanging out with them. They don't have anything. Hey, they're kind of sorry. But you've got us, you've got a family. You know you've got to take care of us. Don't worry about your friends. Worry about us.

Luz and Irma have been together for eight years. Irma has two children from a previous marriage and Luz and Irma have two children together. The family has been involved with Avance for three years. Luz is active in the fatherhood program and was named Father of the Year this year.

LUZ: The reason we fell in love with Avance is they treated us like a family, and like friends. They did not treat us like a client or a complete stranger, they showed us they cared and they wanted to help . . . They helped me to look at myself: what I did then and what I'm doing now and what I want to do later . . . Now I want more for my future.

LUZ: I used to get mad and scream . . .
Spank them without even stopping and
thinking about it. And then [Avance]
showed me about this five-minute time
out. You know, take a break and then
come back and think about what you
were doing. I learned that from them.
I learned how to communicate with my
wife without getting mad and stomping
around the house and getting all drunk
and then coming back . . . With Avance
I also learned how to just sit down, calm
down, turn around, behave and . . . .
I don't storm out of the house no more.
I got it through my thick skull to control
my anger.

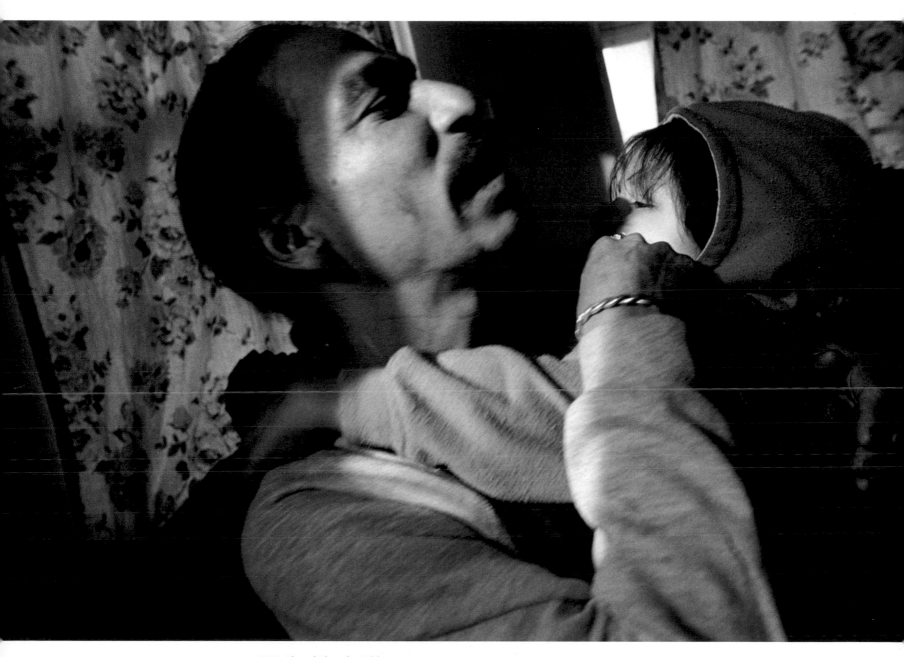

LUZ: I love kids. I don't like to see my kids cry, even when I get mad at them and I punish them. When they start crying, I have to go pick them up.

Next page:
Luz and Irma had a formal wedding ceremony this summer.

LUZ: I don't call it a miracle, I don't call it a God's blessing . . . I call it a bond that will never leave from my heart, 'cause I'm gonna marry this woman and she is gonna take care of me so I gotta do the best I can to have her happy. I think we realized how much we meant to each other on our own . . . We built a bond with each other . . . Avance did a lot for us by making us realize that no goal is greater than what we feel toward each other and what we want to do later in the future.

CASEY COUNTY FAMILY RESOURCE AND YOUTH SERVICES CENTERS

Building the new youth and community center in Liberty, Kentucky, is the bluegrass equivalent of a barn-raising. Until this fall, rural Casey County had no place for teens to get together and engage in safe, fun activities. Marilyn Coffey and Steve Sweeney, coordinators of the Family Resource and Youth Services centers, marshaled resources to address this community need. Local churches held pancake breakfasts and other events to raise money for the center. Through their pastor, Coffey and Sweeney got in touch with a national group, Disciples of Christ Men, who were looking for a work project. Men from Kentucky, Indiana, and Missouri came to help build the youth center. One local gate manufacturing business donated two days of its employees' labor. Women's groups from local churches provided lunches for volunteers.

Consistently acting to meet community needs earns the Family Resource and Youth Services centers credibility in the eyes of folks in Casey County.

CASEY COUNTY FAMILY RESOURCE AND YOUTH SERVICES CENTERS' STORY

Liberty, Kentucky, on the fringes of Appalachia, is typical of rural communities all over the U.S. Family farms have all but disappeared; local merchants have closed up shop, not able to compete with the WalMart in a nearby city; schools over a wide area have been consolidated; people travel to jobs outside the county if they cannot find work at a local steel gate manufacturer or sawmill, or at the Oshkosh B'Gosh embroidering plant. Many subsist by doing odd jobs and seasonally cutting, hanging, and sorting tobacco. Liberty is a small town on the shoulder of a big highway. It has no bowling alley, movie theater, train station, bus stop, or supermarket. There are, however, churches of many denominations, schools, fast food restaurants, and Casey County's Family Resource and Youth Services centers.

"It's hard for folks to concentrate on the fact that their child can't spell or needs help with writing," says Marilyn Coffey, the family resource center's coordinator, "When they're dealing with how to survive from today to tomorrow and how to have food on the table, clothes on their children's backs, a roof over their heads, and medical care."

Communities across Kentucky have family resource and youth services centers because of the Kentucky Education Reform Act of 1990, which sought to improve children's school performance by "removing non-academic barriers to school success." Kentucky's entire public educational system had been ruled unconstitutional because it disadvantaged poor children. In addition to changing the way schools were funded, the Act provided a family resource or youth services center in every school district in which at least 20 percent of the children qualified for free lunches. To promote children's school success, these centers may offer a range of resources including: childcare; training for day-care providers; opportunities for adults to learn about parenting and to gain literacy skills; and referrals for health care, social services, and counseling.

There is also the work of re-creating a lost sense of community. "We grew up in a Norman Rockwell world in the '50s. It just ain't like that anymore," says Steve Sweeney, coordinator of the youth services center. "We're instilling a sense of kinship in the county, the feeling that we're all in this together."

"We're weaving a tapestry here, but at first there were no threads," says Marilyn Coffey. "We don't have the housing that we need. We don't have a transportation system. In many cases we can't refer folks to things, because there aren't things to refer them to. . . . What we do is to look past the barriers and try to figure out ways we can help the community to create resources." In Casey County, this means creating more childcare; bringing church congregations and others together to build a youth and community center; advocating for families to get them housing and Head Start services; and encouraging people to help their neighbors, in part by setting an example.

On a shoestring budget that precludes intensive or comprehensive services, the centers also help children, youth, and families deal with the challenges that accompany poverty. Steve Sweeney, who left a career running his own profitable business, says his current work is more rewarding. "We heard about a girl with cervical cancer who wouldn't go to the doctor," he remembers. "She owed him $800 and she couldn't pay. We couldn't get her a medical card which would let her go for free, because she was underage and Medicaid had a rule that her parents needed to sign her up, and they refused." Sweeney talked to her parents, who were intransigent, and then argued with the local Medicaid office to make an exception to their rule. After many discussions, Medicaid gave the girl a card and covered her expenses retroactively.

"Now she's fine," says Sweeney in a soft, matter-of-fact tone. While not always so direct or dramatic, the work of Kentucky's Family Resource and Youth Service centers is about saving lives.

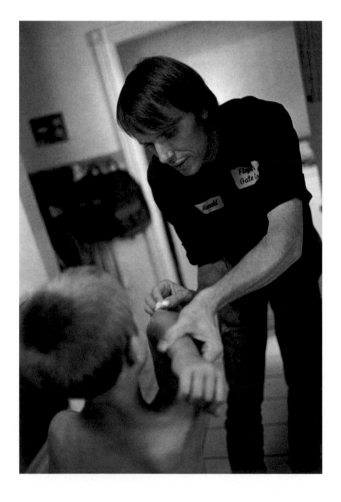

"Pure and simple, if it wasn't for the after-school program, I'd be on welfare,"
says Ron Howard, a single father.

The staff of the Family Resource and Youth Services Center, working with area churches, were instrumental in bringing Habitat for Humanity to Casey County. Ron Howard, single father of three, is the owner of Casey County's first Habitat house. Howard (pictured above in the kitchen of that home with two of his children and a family friend) works in shipping and receiving at the local OshKosh factory.

"Linda's like a sister to me—only better than my sister because she doesn't tell me what to do," says Carolyn Coleman, pictured above and left with her son Matthew and parent educator Linda Sallee. "She doesn't judge me. She just listens and gives me information and ideas."

For parents who want to learn more about child development and are looking for ways to help their young children learn and prepare for school, the family resource center offers home visiting using the Parents as Teachers model. Many of the mothers whom Linda Sallee visits in rural Kentucky don't have neighbors close by or any other contact or support outside their immediate families, so Linda becomes not only a source of information, but a shoulder to cry on and someone to talk to.

Left: After-school program at Liberty Elementary School.

"If families are going to get off welfare and get jobs, there has to be safe, regulated childcare," says Marilyn Coffey, coordinator of the family resource center. "Just building that system within the county has taken a lot of our time. Childcare is the number one need for families in our ten-county area. Back in 1991, when we started, we had twenty-four day-care slots, no infant care, no school-age care in the county. Now, five years later, we have forty school-age childcare slots, sixty preschool and infant-care slots." These "slots" were created by establishing an after-school day care program at the local elementary school and by helping local mothers acquire training to start or expand day-care programs in their homes.

Ron Howard (pictured previously on pages 66 and 67 in his Habitat for Humanity home) uses the subsidized after-school day care for his three children. "Pure and simple, if it wasn't for this program, I'd be on welfare. I'm a single father, if there's no place for my kids to go after school, or if I can't afford what there is, how am I going to work?"

Right: Health care is also hard to come by in Casey County. In response, the youth services center has arranged for a public health nurse to provide physical exams and health screenings for children at the school. The center is able to provide other family members with referrals to health care providers.

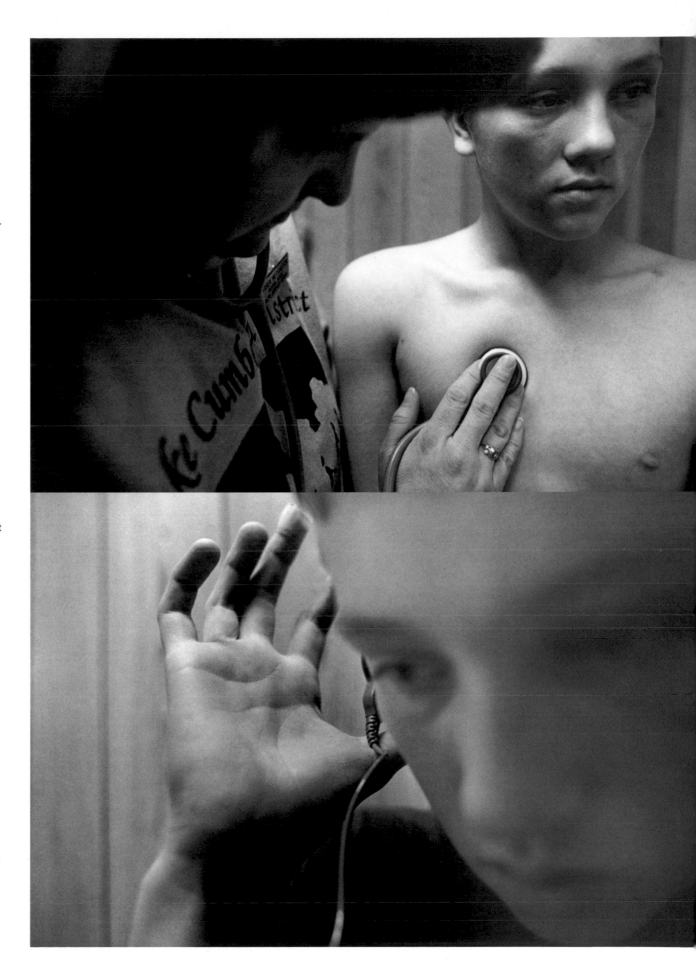

Top left: Richard Crawley and his common-law wife, Violet Hodge, attend a parent involvement meeting at the Middleburg School at which parents and teachers explored how they could better work together to benefit children.

Bottom left: Violet helps Richard's two sons, Richard, Jr., and Bryan with their homework.

Top right: Richard, Jr., fishing.

Bottom right: Richard, with his kids, taking a break from work clearing a field.

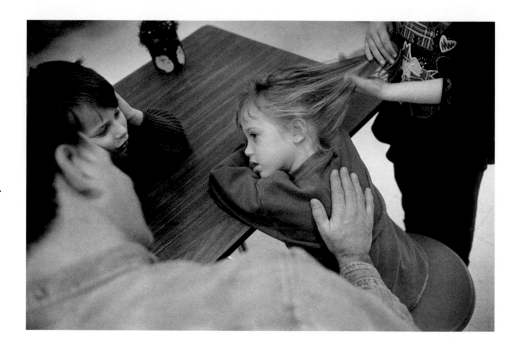

Jeff and Cindy Dean have six children. Cindy now works at WalMart. Last season, Jeff worked as a day-laborer cutting tobacco (previous page) and doing other odd jobs. Like many family resource center participants, Cindy and Jeff don't think of themselves as clients of a state-funded agency. They think of Marilyn and Steve as friends, not as employees of the state education department: "That's Casey County. People here are proud and they're private," says Marilyn Coffey. "If folks thought of us as an agency, it wouldn't work."

JEFF: I'm not rightly sure how we met Marilyn. I think Cindy's the one who met her first. And then Marilyn came over to the house to talk to Cindy and that's how I met her. She's one of the nicest people you could possibly get to know. And she's really bent over backward for us. Back when Cindy and I was both unemployed, Marilyn showed up one day with three bags of groceries. She's been a real pillar of strength.

CINDY: She helped us get our car on the road. She helped us get our kids into after-school day care so we could both work. We used her as a reference so we could get our jobs. Marilyn's a resource for just about anything you need or have questions about; she can give you answers. Marilyn's there if you need to talk.

Part of "being there for people" is helping out in times of emergency. When the Deans' only source of drinking water—their well—clogged, Steve Sweeney, coordinator of the youth services center, called Homer Hecht, a local minister, and they both came out to help Jeff fix it.

COMMUNITY DEVELOPMENT PROGRAMS

TIERRA WOOLS

More than two hundred years ago, Mexicans emigrating to the Chama River Valley of rural New Mexico brought with them herds of Churro sheep, which were to be their livelihood. By the early 1970s, the sheep—whose low-grease wool retains color longer than most wools—were nearly extinct, and the people's shepherding, wool growing, and weaving traditions had almost vanished. Most of the Valley's young people moved away, leaving behind their elders to survive the Valley's extremely harsh winters.

In the early 1980s, Antonio Manzanares, owner of a local sheep farm, Maria Varela, an activist and community organizer, and Gumercindo Salazar, a local teacher, started Ganados Del Valle (Flocks of the Valley) to build from the Chama Valley's traditional way of life and improve the standard of living, empower the community, and preserve its culture and traditions.

The members of the Tierra Wools cooperative run the entire weaving process from beginning to end: raising sheep; shearing them and spinning the wool into yarn; dying the yarn; and weaving the tapestries, blankets—based on traditional Rio Grande patterns—pillows, or clothing to sell in Tierra Wools' local boutique and through its catalog. The Ganados Del Valle development program also includes a livestock shares program for new ranchers, a breeding program to improve flocks, a cooperative grazing program to reduce ranchers' costs, and an intern program for young ranchers. It helps local people start and run businesses such as Pastores Lamb (which sells meat to restaurants, butcher shops, and individuals); Pastores Feed and General Store; the Rio Arriba Wool Washing Plant; and Pastores Collection which explores innovative ways to use wools.

Tierra Wools and Ganados Del Valle have brought economic power and self-respect to the people of the Chama River Valley. People once written off as unskilled, incapable, and destined to live out their lives in hopeless poverty are now running businesses, creating works of art, programming computers, and working to insure their community's survival.

"My mind is different now, it's more open and clear. Before I felt my life was all it could be. Now I know I can do anything," says Anna Cuevas, a home health care worker.

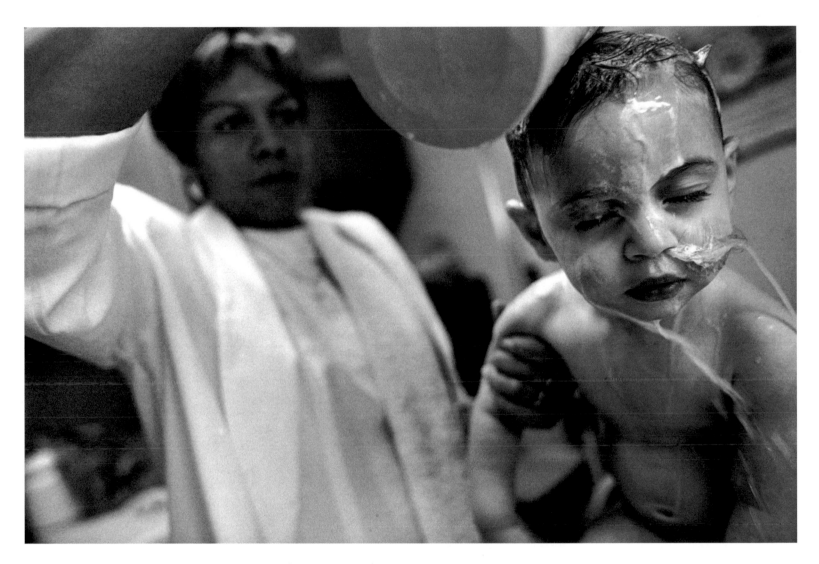

COOPERATIVE
HOME CARE ASSOCIATES
In 1985, when changes in Medicare moved thousands of patients from hospital beds to home, the Community Service Society of New York formed Cooperative Home Care Associates, the nation's largest worker-owned low-income new business, to raise the quality of home health care by improving the working conditions and salaries of home health workers. Located in the South Bronx, CHCA employs more than three hundred African-American and Latina women, many of them former welfare recipients with limited education, skills, and proficiency in English, by training them to become Medicare-certified home health aides—assisting with bathing, grooming, and meal preparation.

Government regulators, union officials, health care administrators, and patient groups have all recognized the outstanding care provided by CHCA employees. With grants from private foundations, health-care cooperatives based on CHCA's example have been created in Boston and Philadelphia, applying the same successful principles: careful selection of new employees, emphasis on individual responsibility, and personalized and supportive counseling and skills training.

Above: Anna Cuevas bathes Stanley, a fragile thirteen-month-old baby who was born missing a heart valve and has undergone several operations. Cuevas, a married mother of four from the Dominican Republic, joined CHCA in 1993 and was elected to its board of directors two years later.

MARSHALL HEIGHTS COMMUNITY DEVELOPMENT ORGANIZATION, INC.

Marshall Heights is one of Washington, D.C.'s most impoverished African-American neighborhoods. In 1983, a group of residents, neighborhood leaders, and representatives of business and government founded the Marshall Heights Community Development Organization (MHCDO), a non-profit organization, to improve housing, make the streets safer, and build hope by attracting new businesses and creating jobs in Marshall Heights and surrounding neighborhoods.

MHCDO is now booming. One of its subsidiaries owns 40 percent of a shopping center (which includes a 62,000-square-foot Safeway grocery). Another acquires, rehabs, and sells single-family homes and rentals. A third MHCDO subsidiary started a local industrial park with 90,000 square feet of inexpensive flexible space for incubating small businesses, including a printing supply company, a courier service, and a metal fabricator. Many of these activities are partially subsidized by grants from the federal government and private foundations.

Michael Morton, manager of business development services for MHCDO, says, "We work with businesses to help them overcome their problems, so that banks will give them loans. For example, Mr. Alston [pictured in front of his take-out restaurant with Morton] never had a bank account. We took him to the bank to set up an account. That's what we do. We show people how to fill out forms, how to keep their books, how to manage their businesses so they make a profit. We helped Mr. Alston get his business on a sound basis so that we could make him a loan. This is not charity work—we want our small businesses to make money—but it really is God's work."

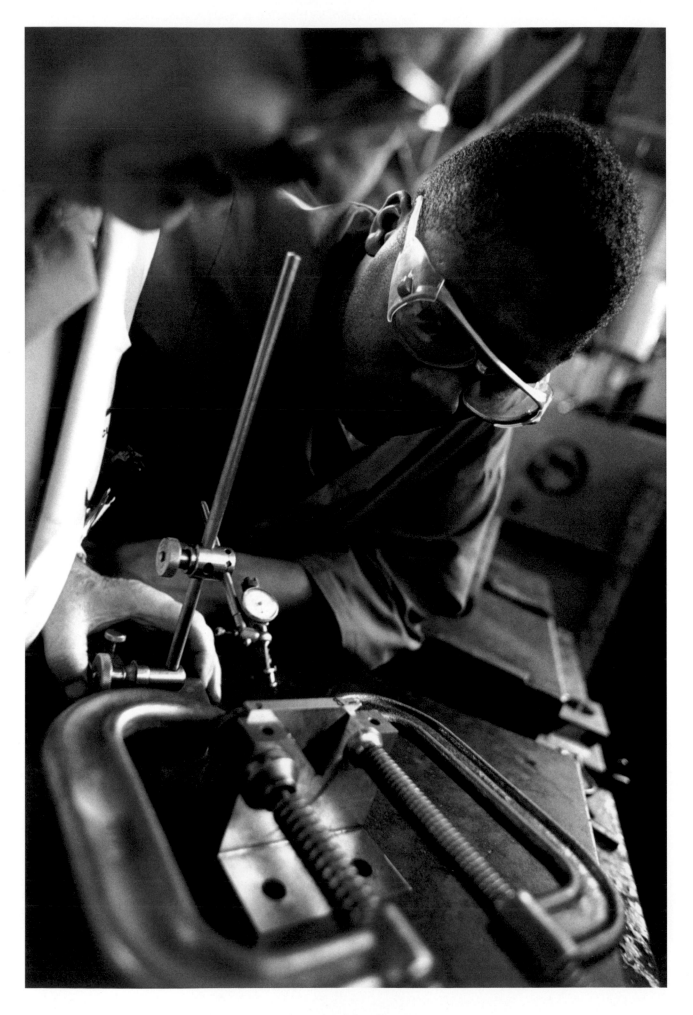

FOCUS: HOPE

In the aftermath of Detroit's 1967 race riots, an interracial movement of volunteers called Focus: Hope was founded to undertake "intelligent and practical action to overcome racism, poverty, and injustice, and to build a metropolitan community." Today, with government, corporate, and foundation support, Focus: Hope employs more than 850 people and involves more than 47,000 volunteers, contributors, and participants.

Besides distributing food to more than 65,000 low-income people annually, Focus: Hope works to rebuild the manufacturing base and to tailor education to market needs. It operates for-profit companies that manufacture vacuum harnesses, hydraulic hoses, a variety of automotive parts, and pulleys. Focus: Hope's accredited Machinist Training Institute is a one-year training program in precision machining and metalworking, fields that have traditionally been closed to blacks, women, and other minorities. All graduates are either placed in jobs as machinists or apprentices, or go on to earn an associate's, a bachelor's, or a master's degree in engineering through Focus: Hope's Center for Advanced Technologies (CAT). Focus: Hope, with a coalition of six universities and seven key industrial partners, is developing an engineering curriculum for the twenty-first century that will benefit the whole country. CAT's students learn by working on the most advanced computer-integrated flexible manufacturing equipment and systems. Focus: Hope's preschool provides quality early childhood education for children of students at Focus: Hope's programs, agency employees, and others in the community.

Focus: Hope's eight-mile Walk
for Justice, held annually since
1968, brings people together to
demonstrate their commitment
to interracial harmony.

SCHOOL / COMMUNITY
PARTNERSHIPS

**GOOSE ROCK FAMILY
RESOURCE CENTER**
Visiting artist Sherry Burns per-
forms a puppet show at Goose
Rock Elementary School in
Appalachia. "Many of our kids
are from isolated hollows in
rural Kentucky. They need experiences. We bring the outside
world to them in any way we
can," says Penny Robinson,
director of the local school-
linked family resource center.

DENVER FAMILY RESOURCE SCHOOLS

A parent volunteer gathers fourth graders to leave for a field trip at Fairview Elementary School, one of Denver's eleven Family Resource Schools. They are open after school and on weekends as community centers, offering programs, such as: 1) after school enrichment to promote student achievement and growth; 2) adult basic education and skill building (GED classes, English as a Second Language classes, and workshops on such issues as housing and employment); 3) parenting education; and 4) family support services to help families reduce non-academic barriers to success in school, such as hunger and lack of heat in the home.

Left: The National Society of Black Engineers sponsors a Rocket Club at Stedman Elementary School.

FAMILY FOCUS LAWNDALE

Family Focus Lawndale is a family support agency that has for fifteen years worked with families in North Lawndale, an impoverished African-American neighborhood in Chicago. Parenting programs at its center are overseen by director Gilda Ferguson and a committed staff of sixteen child development specialists, home visitors, and program assistants— many of whom live in the area and are former program participants. Residents of Lawndale have come to trust Family Focus. They know that the center will collaborate in any initiative or activity that promises to improve conditions for families or to promote a sense of neighborhood belonging. Its efforts to connect pregnant women with prenatal care have cut the community's infant mortality rate in half; it was once the second highest in Illinois.

One of Family Focus's strongest partners is Dvorak Elementary School. Family Focus donates some of its staff members' time to work at the school with Dvorak's parent coordinator, offering parents advice, services, and referrals to other community agencies. Together they also organize parenting workshops, support groups, and joint activities, and they help Dvorak parents to mobilize an active group of volunteers.

Right: A member of Dvorak Elementary School's Parent Patrol helps children walk safely to school and back.

Orientation day for parent volunteers at Dvorak Elementary School in the North Lawndale neighborhood of Chicago.

Peer mediators try to resolve conflicts between students on John Marshall Elementary School's playground. Sixth graders are trained in conflict resolution and intergroup relations. When their efforts cannot neutralize a situation, they call on an adult to help break up the fight. In this case, the instigating student, Deonte, and his family were involved in family counseling through the school; after the fight, their counselor, a graduate student at San Diego State, conducted a therapy session at the school (pages 100-101). A year later, Deonte and his family are still in therapy. He is doing much bettter in school, according to his teacher and the school guidance counselor.

JOHN MARSHALL
ELEMENTARY SCHOOL
is located in one of San Diego's poorest, most transient, and most culturally diverse neighborhoods. Each month forty students enroll and thirty students (out of nine hundred in the entire school) transfer out. Ninety percent of students qualify

for free or reduced-price school lunches. There are more than twenty different language and cultural groups in the school including: Cambodian, Hmong, Lao, Mexican, Salvadoran, Colombian, Vietnamese, and Somali; 68 percent of students speak a language other than English.

In the late 1960s, James Comer, a Yale professor, developed a plan for improving inner-city schools. Suggesting that ghetto children and their parents are often "at odds" with their schools, Comer's view was that no education could succeed until parents and teachers worked together to give children the same messages. The John Marshall Elementary School is one of 165 schools

across the country that adopted the Comer model. Administrators, teachers, support staff, and parents together plan the school's academic, social, and staff development program. The three guiding principles of a Comer school are: no fault, decision making by consensus, and collaboration.

PARENT SERVICES PROJECT encourages child care centers to become family care centers by offering opportunities for parents to form support groups; attend parenting classes, workshops, and adult-only activities; and by hosting family fun events.

Left: Parent Services Project at the Fairfax-San Anselmo Children's Center in Marin County, California, makes special efforts to involve fathers. After a Saturday morning pancake breakfast, fathers and their children prepare to do maintenance work at the center.

For more than twenty years, the Parent Services Project at Fairfax-San Anselmo Children's Center has sponsored a Get Well Room for children up to ten years of age who are too sick to go to school, but not seriously ill. Parents who other- wise might have to lose income (or in some cases even jobs) staying home to care for a sick child can instead drop off their child in a relax- ing, living-room-like environment, assured that she will be well cared for by a qualified staffer.

EXTENDED SCHOOL PROGRAM
(ESP), a public/private partnership in
Murfreesboro, Tennessee, allows
parents to work, knowing that their
kids are involved in supervised
activities and not hanging around an
empty house or a mall or street
corner, where they might get into
trouble. Tennessee's legislature and
the local school district make public
school facilities available rent-free to
ESP's before- and after-school
programming; the district's parents
pay for and help to run the program.

ESP keeps Murfreesboro's nine
elementary schools open year-round
from 6 a.m. to 6 p.m. (including
on snow days and teacher in-service
days) and uses all of the schools'
facilities and equipment—labs,
libraries, music rooms, cafeterias,
and gyms—for music, art, and dance
lessons; computer and foreign language clubs; sports; typing classes;
and scouting programs. Tutors from
Middle Tennessee State University,

classroom teachers, and parent volunteers help students with their homework. Half the district's students
through eighth grade participate.

"The kids have a sense of owner-
ship because they have a say in what
activities we should offer," says Becci
Bookner, ESP's founding director.
"Older kids take karate lessons, do
science projects, play all types of
sports—even horseback riding—
and do other things which give them
a sense of responsibility, like mentoring younger kids."

Next page:
An after-school dance class at
the Extended School Program in
Murfreesboro, Tennessee.

YOUTH DEVELOPMENT PROGRAMS

BRESEE YOUTH
Students at Bresee Youth center remove nearly 10,000-square-feet of graffiti each month through a program sponsored by the city of Los Angeles. Many of the youths do this work as volunteers, with the proceeds going to Bresee.

Right: Soon after this picture was taken, this youth stopped painting so as not to disturb—or spatter paint on—the sleeping homeless man.

The South Central and Mid-Wilshire neighborhoods in Los Angeles have the highest gang-related crime rate in the city, with ten thousand gang members and sixty different gangs. Schools in these communities report drop-out rates as high as 80 percent. There are virtually no parks or recreational facilities. Bresee Youth offers hope to young people, providing adult role models, opportunities, and experiences.

"The biggest problem in our area are those basically good kids on the borderline, who, with support, will choose life, but without support will become victims of the environment they live in," says Jeff Carr, Bresee's director.

Bresee concentrates on education and employment. Former graffiti artists are employed in a computer design and desktop publishing business creating logos, brochures, and flyers for area businesses. Bresee's employment service helps students find part-time work and employs them in its flyer distribution service, its computer lab, and in the

Center's store, as well as hiring them to serve as peer tutors.

At Bresee's homework lab, volunteer mentors and peer tutors help students with reading, writing, and math skills. By attending the lab, students earn points that can be used as currency in the Bresee store. Bresee introduces students to the possibility of attending college, through SAT preparation courses, college tours, and scholarships.

Left: Bresee offers sports and recreational programs, summer field trips, picnics, and wilderness experiences.

Above: At the Bresee store, an employee electronically scans a student's I.D. card to determine how many points he has on account and whether he has credit privileges. The store's credit system was initiated and designed by students, who decided that academic performance would be the best indicator of whether their peers were good credit risks.

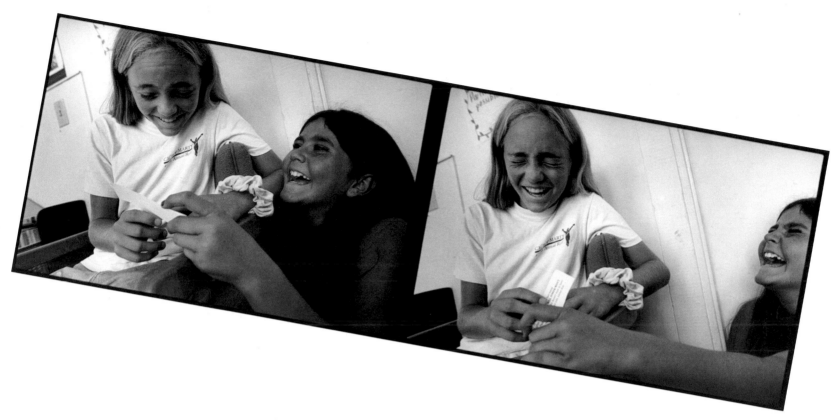

GIRLS, INC.

(formerly Girls Club of America) is a national organization dedicated to helping girls become "strong, smart, and bold." More than half of the girls between the ages of six and eighteen served through its 750 national affiliates are from single-parent, low-income families of all ethnic groups.

One of Girls, Inc.'s main goals is to prevent teenage pregnancy: a recent study found that girls who completed its pregnancy prevention program were half as likely to get pregnant as the general teen population. The program stresses a dual message: abstention is everyone's right and is the best choice, but any teen who does have sex should use both effective contraception and a latex condom to prevent disease.

The entire pregnancy prevention program costs only $127 per girl per year.

Girls, Inc. believes that young girls need to learn about their bodies and to share concerns about sexuality with caring adults; as they get older they need to acquire strong value systems and the skills to make firm decisions and still be popular. The program encourages early communication between parents and their girls, teaches assertiveness through role playing sexual situations (photos above), connects girls to community-based health programs, and attempts to offer alternatives to sex and pregnancy through education and career planning. Girls who have ambitions and plans for their futures, Girls, Inc. has found, are far more likely to delay child-bearing.

Girls, Inc. offers girls who live surrounded by violence and despair a place to be safe. In this neighborhood, gang members regularly accost and grope girls on their way to school.

Left: Girls, Inc. provides a supportive environment and structured time for teens to talk and to advise, comfort, and support each other facilitated by a professionally qualified adult.

Right: Girls, Inc. encourages girls to explore their full potential: to participate in sports, to persist in science and math, and to have a good time.

FOSTER GRANDPARENT PROGRAM
Since 1977, the Foster Grandparent Program in Portland, Maine, has enlisted senior citizens for one-to-one support and nurturing of students in classrooms; for work with troubled adolescents at the Maine Youth Center; to form loving relationships with critically ill children at Maine Medical Center; to provide in-home support to pregnant and parenting teens and other families; and to assist children with special needs in day care, preschool, and Head Start programs. Elders commit twenty hours per week to being a stable, loving presence in a child's life; in return, they receive transportation, meal allowances, accident and liability insurance, an annual physical exam, and a tax-free stipend, as well as the opportunity to share their life experiences and to feel needed.

Left: Matt, an only child who has lost both sets of his grandparents, visits his foster grandmother, Polly Carmichael, at the farm that has been in her family for three generations. During these weekly visits, Polly teaches Matt about the care and feeding of animals.

"Love facilitates growth. The essence of Friends is teaching how to love and how to be lovable, not only in terms of attitudes but also behaviors. Before any strategy to enhance a child's ability to manage his life can begin, he needs to trust this person [his Friend], trust that this is a person who will not harm him. I don't know if it allows them to transcend, but what it does do is unlock their hearts, it opens their minds," says Friends of the Children director Mike Forzley. Friends of the Children gives troubled children "aunts" and "uncles:" committed, full-time mentors from their own community.

FRIENDS OF THE CHILDREN

FRIENDS OF THE CHILDREN'S STORY

In the late 1960s, Duncan Campbell and Mike Forzley were fresh out of college and working in the juvenile court system in Portland, Oregon. Both came to the same conclusion: the vast majority of the kids they saw each day would not be in trouble if each child had had a one-on-one relationship with a caring adult. Coming from a troubled family himself, Campbell vowed that he would change things for other children if he ever became prosperous. By 1993, Campbell was president of a successful investment company. That year, he started Friends of the Children, and hired his old friend Forzley to run the program.

With the help of local elementary schools, Friends of the Children identifies first-graders from the city's most impoverished and dangerous neighborhoods who at that young age already have had problems such as violent or disruptive behavior, truancy, despondency, or poor academic performance, or who teachers suspect are being abused or neglected at home. Then it pairs each of these children with a full-time, paid mentor from the community. Each adult "Friend" is responsible for eight children. "We want people who really care about children," says Forzley. "We hire committed people and pay them good salaries," as opposed to relying on the good will of volunteers, he says. The program promises to stay with each child through high-school graduation. Like surrogate aunts and uncles, Friends offer children love and guidance and support; they also offer these children opportunities that they otherwise would not have. Forzley says, "We become their window to the world beyond their neighborhood."

A Friend can be a tremendous source of relief and support for a struggling parent. "We have a philosophy that says that the parents, no matter where they are in their lives, are doing the best job they can under the circumstances. . . . Pretty soon the parents realize 'This person is not here to take away my kid. This person is not going to come down on me like all the agencies do.' They start to see the kid improving and they go, 'Wow, it's working'. They see how the Friend acts with their kid. Suddenly the parent has a person who is treating them with dignity and kindness, and pretty soon the parent starts to feel a little different about themselves," says Forzley.

Friends of the Children, however, does not—and sometimes cannot—depend on a parent's active participation. "We become friends of the entire family, but . . . our focus is on the child," says Forzley. Approximately 25 percent of the children Friends work with are being cared for by people other than their parents. Forzley remembers one mother with a severe substance-abuse problem who couldn't get her six-year-old up for school. She repeatedly promised the child's Friend that she'd try; but nothing changed. "Well, to us, the solution is to buy the child an alarm clock, teach him how to get up, teach him how to make his breakfast, teach him how to get himself to school. That's the reality. . . . We have to teach these kids to survive in the families they're in," says Forzley.

Friends of the Children is still too young to have concrete evaluation results, but when the program started, the Northwest Regional Educational Laboratory began an evaluation of Friends participants that will follow them for ten years. In the first four years, Friends have witnessed turnarounds that augur well for the future. Original staff member Zach Harris talks about T.R., "I've seen a great change. There was a time where every day he'd always be hitting somebody. He missed twenty-two days of school because of suspensions two years ago. I think he only had one fight last year." Now, T.R. has begun fourth grade, and Zach says that he "started out the new year fresh, and his teacher had no idea that this was the 'bad kid' that everybody had been talking about, because he was so sweet." T.R. is now helping other children with reading and was recently overheard encouraging a classmate: "Now relax, take a break. When you're ready, we'll try again. I know you can do it."

Mike Madden eats lunch in the school cafeteria with his young friends A.J. and Tony and mediates an argument. Jackie Jones helps Ladondrica with schoolwork.

"Friends are on hand every day. They see their kids in school and after school. Our basic premise is that these kids don't get enough attention, caring, and support," says Mike Forzley, director of Friends of the Children.

When the school district could no longer fund summer school at Lent Elementary School, Friends of the Children raised money from local businesses and provided a half-day program to bring children up to grade level.

"If he didn't have Zach around,
most likely, T.R. would end up
being a gang member,"
says T.R.'s mother, Ivy Brown.

According to T.R.'s Friend, Zach
Harris: "He's going to be the king of
Hell or he's going to be sitting at the
right hand of God. Yup, T.R. has
leadership qualities. Everybody
follows this kid."

"If he didn't have Zach around,
most likely, T.R. would end up being
a gang member," says Ivy Brown,
T.R.'s mother. "Right now he's nine
years old, and he knows a lot of gang
members. By Zach being part of our
lives, he takes T.R. away from the
neighborhood where we live, just to
get a different aspect on life, other
than just drug dealing, gang banging,
and all that stuff. He has taken him to
real basketball games, to the show.
They went out to eat, just to talk.
To the zoo."

T.R. had promised Zach that he would be respectful to his teacher and classmates all day, but he broke his promise. When asked to complete a simple task, T.R. told his teacher, "I ain't doin' nothin'." Zach says, "I walked in the classroom during the middle of his argument with his teacher: I could see the pain in his eyes. He wanted to apologize for letting me down, but it was too late. He was knee-deep into his negative attitude. When I took him outside the room to chat, he expected me to go off on him, but instead, I listened to him complain for twenty minutes, then I embraced him with compassion. It caught him totally off guard."

ZACH: God has given you so many qualities: a beautiful smile, a healthy body, and a high level of intelligence. Only you can make the best of what is given to you. But the teacher is in the class and your butt is out here! Whose fault is that? You're not the only person who's going to make mistakes. You will be something special if you can rise above your mistakes. Just be quick to take responsibility for your own actions. Only men can do that. Are you a man?

TR: Yes.

ZACH: You are not a true man until you go through fire, not around it. So far you've chosen to go around the fire, so that makes you a potential young man. There are quite a few potential young men in prison. Is that where you want to end up?

TR: Naw, man. I ain't goin' to prison.

ZACH: Then keep your butt in the fire.

TR: Okay.

ZACH: A friend is someone who loves you even when you're not at your best. That's who I am. It doesn't matter what you do or how many times you do it wrong. I'm gonna love you just the same. I got your back, man. You really don't have a choice, T.R. Man, you are stuck with me for life. Get that through your head. I'm not going anywhere. Get back in the fire and get your job done, okay? I love you, buddy.

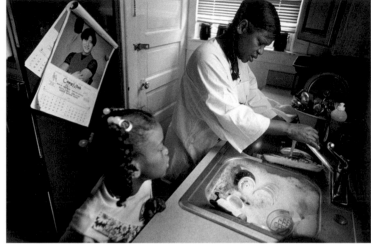

T.R.'s mother, Ivy, says, "When [Friends of the Children] first became a part of our lives, I was on welfare and they were doing a lot of things for T.R., and I was kind of jealous because I wasn't able to give to him as much as they did. . . . And Zach would come over and see all these gin bottles, all these beer cans, like there was a party at my house every night. I felt bad, so I said I need to really just clean up my act. I'm telling him [Zach] what I want to do that's positive, but at the same time, every time he would come over all he would see was negativity. But he just kept coming, no matter what, and doing for my child, not only material, but spending quality time with my child and showing my child love. . . . I just decided that, hey, you know something, you can do better than this. So what I did was I just got up and I got busy. I went and got me a job and they had cut my [welfare] check because of my job, and I wanted more money. So I decided, 'I'll get another job.' I work two jobs so I can be totally off of welfare, and that's what I did because they showed me that they loved and cared for T.R. I said, 'I'm his mother, you know, I had him. And I love him a lot. It's better in the long run for my child if I'm really paying attention to what is going on.' So they influenced me to get up and do something positive with my life."

Each child spends at least five hours a week with his or her Friend, going to the park or the mall or the movies or to get a haircut; getting help with their homework; learning about personal hygiene; or just playing basketball or making brownies together. Many times, the Friend is the person whom the child or his teacher calls in emergencies. A Friend is a constant in the child's life, which otherwise may be full of upheaval and transience. For example, one Friend spent the night with a child at the child protective services agency office, waiting for him to be placed in foster care. Otherwise that child, about to be separated from the only family he had ever known, could have spent that night without anyone he trusted, ostensibly alone.

Jackie Jones with her friend,
Ladondrica, at the mall. "Ladondrica,
she went through a major transfor-
mation. She used to cry so much, it
was just unreal. Every day. She just
didn't feel good about herself, so
everything else around her affected
her. She doesn't do that no more.
She handles the problems more.
Before she goes to someone else,
she tries to handle them first. It took
longer to teach that to her than to
anybody else, but she's grown a lot,"
says Jackie.

Right: Friends Zach and Perry horsing around.

Below: Friends and their kids sacked out on the van ride home from a day-trip to Seattle.

Next page:
Friends participated in Martin Luther King Elementary School's "hug line," a ritual that takes place at the end of every school day in the summer.

PARENTS AND CHILDREN TOGETHER

Once known as the worst housing project in Hawaii, Kuhio Park Terrace (KPT) has over the past few years become "a pretty nice place to live," according to many tenants. The change was brought about by the combined efforts of the development's management; its residents; area police; and a social services agency with a branch at KPT, Parents and Teachers Together (PACT). It couldn't have happened without funding provided by state and federal government.

The Hanalike Home Visitor Program, a twenty-year-old child abuse prevention program (available at KPT through PACT, see page 140) has a phenomenal success rate. Its program has been replicated in Hawaii as Healthy Start and across the Mainland U.S. as Healthy Families America. The following story shows how it works:

Five years ago, after giving birth to her third child, Talo Tufaga, (on left in photo), was visited in the hospital by a worker with ties to Hanalike. The worker determined that, based on Tufaga's background and the stresses in her life, there was a serious risk that she would abuse or neglect her newborn. Hanalike offered help: five years of intensive home visits by a knowledgeable, caring person who would support her emotionally and give her information that she could use to improve her relationship with her children and to achieve her goals for herself. Tufaga agreed.

Since then, she has, according to her Hanalike home visitor Carla Juarez, "made big strides."

Tufaga says, "I changed the way I am raising my kids. I spend more time with them reading, talking, doing things together. I listen to them, what they're feeling. Instead of hitting or spanking or yelling at them, I talk to them and we sort our feelings out. And I noticed a difference when I stopped doing all those things, that [now] we have good communication. It's like they trust me. And they tell me they love me. That never happened before."

In addition, Tufaga has acquired her high school equivalency diploma and she is moving off welfare—working part-time at the PACT Head Start program at KPT (as shown in this photo) and studying to be a draftsman. "I'm going to school. I'm educating myself. I've gotten enough information through Carla's program so I can just build my life and get my life straight," says Tufaga.

"PACT mobilizes parents to volunteer and to act on their own behalf."

KPT's STORY

Honolulu's Kuhio Park Terrace (KPT) is a thirty-year-old, federally funded housing complex for low-income families. Dark, graffiti-covered stairwells smell of urine; unreliable elevators strand tenants in the high-rise buildings; and, in the surrounding areas, there is easy access to methamphetamine, marijuana, crack cocaine, and other drugs. Violence—within and between families—is always on the verge of erupting. KPT is home to 3,800 legal tenants (and an estimated 2,200 unauthorized residents): roughly half are Samoan, and the rest are Native Hawaiian, Filipino, Vietnamese, Chinese, Puerto Rican, African-American, and Caucasian.

Lui Feleafine, the development's manager, recalls that when he first came to KPT in 1981, "all hell would break loose" after dark. The first time he called the police was when two hundred people were going at each other with Samoan cricket bats in KPT's courtyard: a feud between families had gotten out of control. The officers took three hours to respond. Back then, if the police showed up at all, they would park their cars outside the complex to avoid being hit by eggs, ice cubes, batteries, and even refrigerators. Feleafine says, "People had no respect for law. No respect for nobody."

Over time, things at KPT have improved. Residents, police, the housing authority, and social service providers working together have banned drug deals from KPT grounds.

Management increased security and pressured problem tenants and uncooperative guests to move. There is a growing sense of community.

KPT's turnaround is not the result of a single magic bullet, one particular service or strategy, or a sudden quick fix. It is the result of the "good guys" receiving support and resources over a long period of time so that they can tip the balance, get rid of the troublemakers, and win over the fence-sitters.

Two of the strongest allies in KPT's battle have been the federal government and the State of Hawaii. The federal government has passed tough laws (such as the 1985 act that prohibited persons evicted from one federally funded housing project from ever living in any other), and has funded some of the most effective social services for children and families in poverty, including Head Start, W.I.C. (Women, Infants, and Children's nutrition program), Parent-Child Centers, and school meals.

Hawaii became the first state to require that all its citizens be afforded health care. The state's ten-year-old child abuse prevention program, Healthy Start, has a 99 percent success rate and is being replicated across the U.S. Hawaii has long demonstrated a commitment to helping families in poverty overcome obstacles, and residents of KPT have for more than twenty-five years had a range of services available to them on-site, including a medical clinic and several service agencies. One of these agencies, Parents and Children Together (PACT), manages programs including: a Parent-Child Center,

Hanalike Home Visitor Program (the original twenty-year-old child abuse prevention program on which Healthy Start was based), a teen program, and a youth center.

PACT also encourages all those involved with KPT to work together as a community and mobilizes parents to volunteer and to act on their own behalf. PACT also trains and employs KPT residents.

PACT has known for some time, and the state of Hawaii has learned, that simply making some services available to some needy families isn't enough. Services have to be coordinated and must reach the families who need them. That is why, four years ago, Hawaii funded six family centers at $125,000 each; one of them is located at KPT, managed by PACT.

Intended as a "one-stop-shopping" place for all families to be connected with what they need, PACT's family center is also a place for neighbors to get to know each other, to learn about available resources, and to organize to help themselves. Center activities and services are determined by participants. The Family Center has has no eligibility requirements, waiting lists, or restricted number of "slots"; participation is voluntary. The family center is a hub of community activities and a place where service providers talk to each other to coordinate the activities of their agencies.

Just as things seem to be looking up for KPT residents, and social programs such as Healthy Start are proving effective, major cutbacks in federal government support are forcing Hawaii, like other states, to reduce or cap the budgets of many of its social programs. Last summer the state announced plans to cut funding for KPT's family center, and all other state-funded social service programs including Healthy Start, by 50 to 90 percent.

KPT residents responded by organizing an island-wide "Save the Family Centers Rally." Helenann Lauber, director of the PACT Family Center, says, "The rally was the community's effort to save us. We invited the world: Congresspeople, Senators, everybody. Letters from our Congressmembers were read at the rally. A local public television station did a thirty-minute report on the cuts and showed it three times. We had stories in all the newspapers and circulated petitions." In addition, residents and their children met individually with state legislators, including the Speaker of the House, and testified at public hearings. The same courtyard that was once the scene of riots between neighbors became the stage for unified, collaborative, and purposeful action.

In the wake of state funding cuts, PACT was able to cobble together funds from other sources to keep the family center going. So, for now, funding for PACT's programs is intact, the courtyard is quiet, and the good guys are winning. But there, as elsewhere, when there is progress it is vulnerable, when there is peace it is fragile.

PACT's Parent-Child Center, one of twenty-six such centers funded by the federal government since 1970, can only accommodate one in every thirty-six of the families who apply to participate. Now linked with Head Start (the nation's most successful early childhood education program for three- and four-year-olds from low-income families), the Center provides early childhood education for infants and toddlers. PACT also offers parenting classes and a respite child care program, which allows parents to leave their young children at the center twice a week for up to three hours at no charge.

"When I first came [to PACT], I was a mom with no patience. And I expected my baby to act like a four- or five-year-old. I didn't really know that much. I thought that when I said, 'Be quiet,' the baby should be quiet," says Elena Usavale. "I learned a lot. I learned how to be patient. I learned how there's other ways of punishing them without hitting them. Before, all I knew was to hit."

Above: Two children play on a Parent-Child Center picnic at a local park.

Top left: On a field trip to a local supermarket sponsored by PACT's Parent-Child Center, mothers learn about nutrition and how to feed their families healthfully and inexpensively.

Bottom left: KPT's Friendly Store, a grocery/convenience store that also helps KPT tenants develop job skills, was one of the first programs started by Family Center participants. The store has become a gathering place, an informal way for residents to connect with each other and the Family Center. Initially governed by a board of residents (in this photo) and by PACT staff, the store's operation was turned over to three residents in 1996.

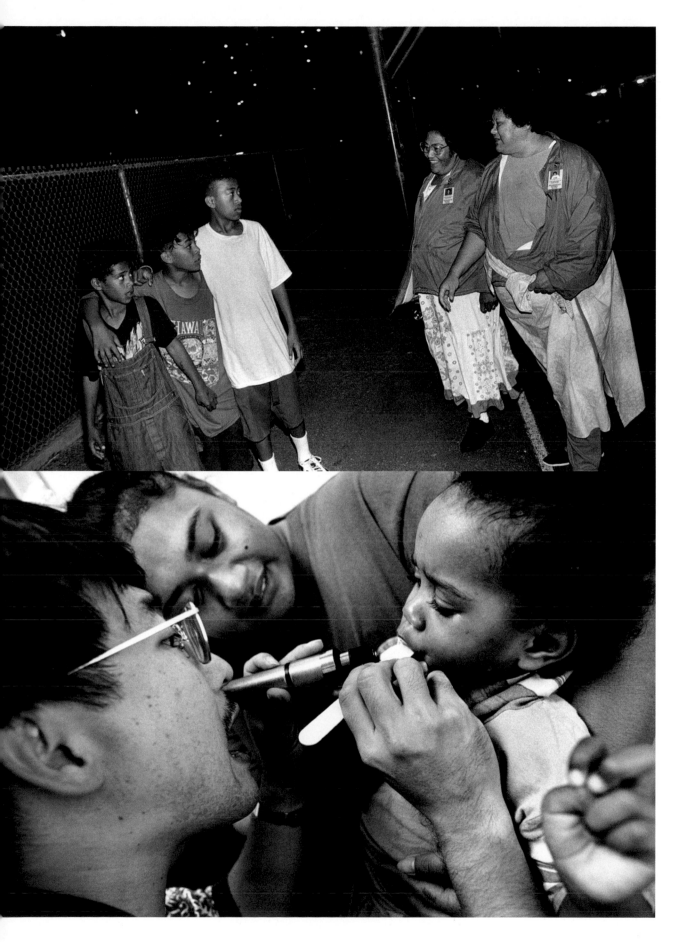

Top right: Through KPT's Family Center, residents organized a Night Watch patrol to help keep KPT safe. Patrollers carry portable radios to reach police; Ene Taifane, one of the organizers of the watch, says, "We just walk and let people know that we're out there, that there's eyes looking at them. If there's a problem, we contact the police or the management staff and they come down and take care of the matter. We're the eyes and ears of the community."

Bottom right: PACT insures that KPT residents have access to medical care through a local health center which is a collaboration between state public health nurses, the Women, Infants, and Children nutrition program, and the Kokua Kalihi Valley Keola Mamo, a member of the Hawaiian Health System. The health center's van brings women to its prenatal and well-baby classes. PACT's "Immunize for a Family Prize" program provided food packages from the KPT Friendly Store for families who had had their young children fully vaccinated.

Left: The Pei family started their small business, a lunch wagon, with a loan and technical advice from the PACT Family Center's microenterprise program.

Right: Lemina Sufia, a former Hanalike participant, was able to start an in-home day care program with training and support from PACT's Family Child Care Network. She cares for five toddlers, including her own son.

PACT manages a youth center at KPT where kids go to get help with homework and to participate in a variety of arts and sports programs and community service activities— alternatives to hanging out in gangs. One worker says, "They have a lot of trouble with gangs here. Once every three or four months somebody used to go falling off the roof of one of the buildings. . . . [Now] they're trying to do things with the older kids, basketball and crafts and silk screening T-shirts and stuff, just to get them out of the area."

Linapuni Elementary School, across the street from KPT, is a nationally acclaimed "blue ribbon" school for kindergarten through second-grade students. Parents and community members, including PACT staff, are involved in all levels of the school's management, from helping to define curriculum goals to volunteering in classrooms and planning community celebrations. PACT encourages parents to come to school with their children.

"I look at our school as a place of hope for the community," says Linapuni Principal Dennis Dobies.

"It's so difficult for any one of our adults to break the cycle. I don't see them getting out of here mostly. But there's a chance for their kids. And as long as we give their kids the best of everything and the best education possible, then they can have dreams that will come true."

"As long as we give our kids the best of everything and the best education possible, then they can have dreams that will come true."

Left: A mother and father watch their children work on computers at Linapuni Elementary School.

Above: A classroom at Linapuni.

PACT's Parent-Child Center encourages parents to read to their children and regularly takes mothers and their children to the local library.

PROGRAM LISTING

ALGEBRA PROJECT, INC.
99 Bishop Allen Drive
Cambridge, MA 02139
617-491-0200
Fax: 617-491-0499
Contact: Robert Moses

ASPECTS PROGRAM
Tripler Army Medical Center
Honolulu, HI 96859-5000
808-433-1604
Fax: 808-433-1615
Contact: JoEllen Cerny

AVANCE FAMILY SUPPORT
AND EDUCATION PROGRAM
301 South Frio Street (#310)
San Antonio, TX 78207
210-270-4630
Fax: 210-270-4612
Contact: Carmen Cortez, VP

BEDFORD STUYVESANT VOLUNTEER
AMBULANCE CORPS
727 Green Avenue
Brooklyn, NY 11221
718-453-4617
Fax: 718-452-2123
Contact: James (Rocky) Robinson

BRESEE YOUTH
3401 West Third Street
Los Angeles, CA 90020
213-387-2822
Fax: 213-385-8482
E.mail: jcarr@bresee.com
Jeff Carr, Executive Director

CASEY COUNTY FAMILY RESOURCE
CENTER
1922 N. U.S. 127
Liberty, KY 42539
606-787-7985
Contact: Marilyn Coffey,
Coordinator

CASEY COUNTY YOUTH SERVICES
CENTER
1922 N. U.S. 127
Liberty, KY 42539
606-787-6566
Contact: Steve Sweeney,
Coordinator

CENTER FOR FAMILY LIFE IN
SUNSET PARK
345 43rd Street
Brooklyn, NY 11232
718-788-3500
Contacts: Sisters Mary Geraldine
and Mary Paul Janchill, Directors

CENTER FOR INTERGENERATIONAL
LEARNING
Temple University
206 University Services Blvd.
1601 N. Broad Street
Philadelphia, PA 19122
215-204-6836
Fax: 215-204-6733
Contact: Nancy Henkin, Director

COOPERATIVE HOME CARE
ASSOCIATES
349 East 149th Street
Bronx, NY 10451
718-993-7104
Fax: 718-665-6008
Contact: Rick Surpin

DENVER FAMILY RESOURCE
SCHOOLS
1330 Fox Street
Denver, CO 80204
303-405-8189
Contact: Bruce Atchison, Director

EARLY EDUCATION SERVICES
30 Birge Street
Brattleboro, VT 05301
802-254-3742
Fax: 802-254-3750
Contact: Judith Jerald, Director

EAST BAY CENTER FOR THE
PERFORMING ARTS
339 11th Street
Richmond, CA 94801
510-234-5624
Fax: 510-234-8206
Contact: Jordan Simmons,
Artistic Director

EXTENDED SCHOOL PROGRAM
400 North Maple Street
PO Box 279
Murfreesboro, TN 37133-0279
615-893-2313
Fax: 615-893-2352
Contact: Peggy Seneker, Director

FACE PROGRAM
Torreon Day School
HCR 79 Box 9
Cuba, NM 87013
505-731-2272
Fax: 505-731-2252
Contact: Sue Neddeau

FAMILY FOCUS LAWNDALE
3333 West Arthington (Suite 108)
Chicago, IL 60624
773-722-5057
Fax: 773-722-5160
Contact: Gilda Ferguson, Director

FOCUS: HOPE
1355 Oakman Blvd
Detroit, MI 48238
313-494-5500
Fax: 313-494-4340
Contact: Donna DiSante

FOSTER GRANDPARENT PROGRAM
284 Danforth Street
Portland, ME 04102
207-773-0202
Fax: 207-874-1155
Contact: Susan Lavigne

FRIENDS OF THE CHILDREN
PO Box 90248
Portland, OR 97290-0248
503-762-4047
Fax: 503-762-1317
Contact: Mike Forzley, Director

GIRLS INCORPORATED OF
ORANGE COUNTY
1835 Newport Blvd.
Suite E-265
Costa Mesa, CA 92627
714-646-7181
Fax: 714-646-5313
Contact: Jo Gottfried

GOOSE ROCK FAMILY RESOURCE
CENTER
Route 7 Box 200
Manchester, KY 40962
606-598-4454
Fax: 606-598-4454
Contact: Penny Robinson,
Coordinator

INSTITUTE FOR RESPONSIBLE
FATHERHOOD AND FAMILY
REVITALIZATION
1146 19th St., NW #800
Washington, D.C. 20036-3703
202-293-4420
Fax: 202-293-4288
Contact: Charles Ballard

JAMES JORDAN BOYS & GIRLS CLUB
AND FAMILY LIFE CENTER
2102 West Monroe
Chicago, IL 60612
312-226-2323
Fax: 312-226-9788
Contact: Lloyd T. Walton,
Club Director

JOHN MARSHALL ELEMENTARY
SCHOOL
3550 Altadena Avenue
San Diego, CA 92105
619-283-5924
Fax: 619-563-4162
Contact: Linda Kocis

KELLY ELEMENTARY SCHOOL
9030 SE Cooper
Portland, OR 97766
503-916-6350
Contact: Fran Eichenauer

MANCHESTER CRAFTSMEN'S GUILD
1815 Metropolitan Street
Pittsburgh, PA 15233
412-322-1773
Fax: 412-321-2120
Contact: Hilary Rose, Director of
Development

MARSHALL HEIGHTS COMMUNITY
DEVELOPMENT ORGANIZATION
3732 Minnesota Avenue, NE
Washington, D.C. 20019
202-397-7300
Contact: Rose Strickland, public
relations

O'FARRELL COMMUNITY SCHOOL
FOR ADVANCED ACADEMIC STUDIES
6130 Skyline Drive
San Diego, CA 92114
619-263-3009
Fax: 619-262-1496
Contact: Mary Skrabucha

PACT PARENTS AND CHILDREN
TOGETHER
1475 Linapuni Street, Suite 117-A
Honolulu, HI 96819
808-847-3285
Fax: 808-841-1485
Contact: Ruthann Quitiquit,
Executive Director

PARENT SERVICES PROJECT
199 Porteous Avenue
Fairfax, CA 94930
415-454-1870
Fax: 415-454-1752
Contact: Ethel Seiderman,
Executive Director

SAN DIEGO POLICE DEPARTMENT
NEIGHBORHOOD POLICING
1401 Broadway
San Diego, CA 92101
619-531-2770
Fax: 619-531-2975
Contact: Asst. Chief John Welter

TIERRA WOOLS
PO Box 229
Los Ojos, NM 87551
Contact: Antonio and Molly
Manzanares

ADVISORY COMMITTEE

Eric Brettschneider, Agenda for Children Tomorrow, New York, New York

Eve Brooks, National Association of Child Advocates, Washington, D.C.

Hedy Nai-Lin Chang, California Tomorrow, San Francisco, California

Jerlean Daniel, University of Pittsburgh, Pittsburgh, Pennsylvania

Frank Farrow, Center for the Study of Social Policy, Washington, D.C.

Marc Freedman, Public/Private Ventures, Philadelphia, Pennsylvania

Darold Johnson, Children's Defense Fund, Washington, D.C.

Judith E. Jones, National Center for Children in Poverty, New York, New York

Deborah Meier, New York Networks for School Renewal, New York, New York

Sonia Perez, National Council of La Raza, Washington, D.C.

Karen Pittman, International Youth Foundation, Baltimore, Maryland

Gene Roberts, *New York Times,* New York, New York

Lisbeth Schorr, Project on Effective Services, Harvard University, Cambridge, Massachusetts

Heather Weiss, Harvard Family Research Project, Cambridge, Massachusetts

APERTURE

Aperture Foundation publishes a periodical, books, and portfolios of fine photography to communicate with serious photographers and creative people everywhere. A complete catalog is available upon request.
Address: 20 East 23rd Street
New York, New York 10010
Phone: 212-598-4205
Fax: 212-598-4015.

The Staff at Aperture for *Pursuing the Dream* is:
Michael E. Hoffman, *Executive Director*
Lois Brown, *Editor*
Stevan A. Baron, *Production Director*
Helen Marra, *Production Manager*
Kara Masciangelo, *Editorial Work-Scholar*
Katie Warwick, *Production Work-Scholar*

FAMILY RESOURCE COALITION

Family Resource Coalition is a national membership, consulting, and advocacy organization that has been advancing the movement to strengthen and support families since 1981. The family support movement and FRC seek to strengthen and empower families and communities so that they can foster the optimal development of children, youth, and adult family members. FRC builds networks, produces resources, advocates for public policy, provides consulting services, and gathers knowledge to help the family support movement grow.

For more information about any of the programs described in this book or about other programs that strengthen families, contact:

Family Resource Coalition
200 S. Michigan Ave., 16th Floor
Chicago, Illinois 60604
Phone: 312-341-0900
Fax: 312-341-9361
E-mail: famres.org

The staff at Family Resource Coalition for *Pursuing the Dream* is:
Virginia Mason, *Executive Director*
Kathy Goetz Wolf, *Project Director*
Jacqueline Lalley, *Copyeditor*
Shelley Peck, *Editor*
Jonathan Wolf, *Editor*
Jennifer Wolff, *Reporter*
Linda Turner, *Fact Checker*
Shamara Riley, *Editorial Assistant*

Family Resource Coalition extends special thanks to former executive director Judy Langford Carter for her leadership and guidance in shaping this project during its formative stages and for her careful review of the final manuscript.

OUTSIDE THE DREAM FOUNDATION

Outside the Dream Foundation (OTDF) is a non-profit organization started in 1995 by photographer Stephen Shames that is dedicated to helping children and their families succeed by using photography to educate the public and create a national will to act on behalf of children.

Outside the Dream Foundation collaborates on projects that demonstrate solutions to problems facing children and families, projects such as this book and a three-year, twenty-city traveling exhibit of the photographs in *Pursuing the Dream,* designed and produced in cooperation with local community programs and accompanied by lectures, seminars, and concerts.

Outside the Dream Foundation will work with individuals and corporations to generate continuing sources of income that will be used to create and distribute photography to educate the public. Within the next several years, OTDF plans include Kid Card, a credit card that will donate a percentage of sales to Outside the Dream Foundation, and For the Children, a compilation music CD. Contact Outside the Dream Foundation at:

423 Atlantic Avenue, 6D
Brooklyn, N.Y. 11217
http://www.thedream.org

ACKNOWLEDGMENTS

Thanks to Janice Molnar and Bob Curvin of the Ford Foundation and Jon Blyth of the Charles Stewart Mott Foundation for helping me to shape this dream, for their personal and financial commitment to this project and for their faith in my vision.

Thanks to Paul Curtis of Eastman Kodak, Dave Metz of Canon, and Cindy Hahn of Leica for years of support and friendship and for providing film and equipment for this project. Thanks to the Pennsylvania Council of the Arts and to Eva Winmoller and Thomas Hopker, Molly Gordy-Drew and Dick Drew, Nick Kelsh, and Barry and Leslie Usow for financial support when I needed it most.

Thanks to the following people, without whose help this book would not have happened.

Marian Wright Edelman suggested I look at solutions.

Phyllis Stoffman visited and researched programs—and has given me a lifetime of affection, friendship, and support.

Kathy Goetz Wolf of the Family Resource Coalition has been a committed partner at all stages of the research, editorial, design, and writing processes. Wendy Byrne at Aperture contributed a fabulous design and exquisite photo sense. Kathy and Wendy took my vision and carried it further; it is their book as much as it is mine.

Lloyd Garrison, Marty Roysher, and Mustafa Abdul Salaam for introducing me to the right people.

Peter, Francine, Stephen, David, and Michael Caputo, Sarah and Reed Phillips, Diana and Steve Strandberg, Hayes Greenfield, David H. Wells, Alen MacWeeney and Hazel Hammond, Heidi Nivling and Larry Becker, Larry Kesterson, Gil Carrasco, and my agents Barbara Sadick and Jonathan Wells of Matrix provided advice, help with picture selection, and moral support. The project's advisory committee members and Bill Treanor, Janet Levy, Judy Langford Carter, Lynn Pooley, Roland Anglin, Mark Elliot, Ron Mincy, Peter Goldmark, Cathy Trost, Donna Jablonski, Marjorie Johnson, and Elena Cabral helped select programs, conceptualize, and frame the project. Alberto Caputo, Sam Erickson, Paula Bullwinkel, Felicia Lopez, Maria Levitzky of Lexington Labs worked hard at making the best possible photographic prints. Michael Hoffman, Lois Brown, Stevan A. Baron, and Kara Masciangelo of Aperture as well as David Friend, Walter Anderson, Rich Folkers, Jimmy Colton, Myra Kreiman, Robert Coles, and Arthur Ollman gave invaluable guidance, technical expertise, and help reaching the public. Jennifer Wolff's interviews and reporting contributed greatly to the text. Thanks to Mary Jean Bartow and Pat Menta for transcribing. Thanks also to Roger Rosenblatt for being part of this project.

I am grateful to all of the programs I visited and to the dedicated individuals who work in them for letting me hang out and watch them reconstruct neighborhoods and help families succeed. They taught me everything you see in this book.

Finally, I want to thank the families I photographed for letting me into their lives and homes. These parents' faith in a better life for their children inspired me to keep going when I got discouraged. They are America's unsung heroes.

—Stephen Shames

EASTMAN KODAK AND CANON, U.S.A., made generous contributions of film and equipment for this project.

Library of Congress Catalog Card Number: 97-070516
Hardcover ISBN: 0-89381-728-7

Book and jacket design by Wendy Byrne

Printed and bound by Marigros Industrie Grafiche SpA, Turin, Italy
Separations by Sele Offset, Turin, Italy

Aperture Foundation publishes a periodical, books, and portfolios of fine photography to communicate with serious photographers and creative people everywhere. A complete catalog is available upon request.
Address: 20 East 23rd Street, New York, New York 10010
Phone: (212) 598-4205
Fax: (212) 598-4015

Aperture Foundation books are distributed internationally through:

CANADA:
General Publishing,
30 Lesmill Road, Don Mills, Ontario, M3B 2T6.
Fax: (416) 445-5991.

UNITED KINGDOM:
Robert Hale, Ltd.,
Clerkenwell House, 45-47 Clerkenwell Green, London EC1R OHT.
Fax: 171-490-4958.

CONTINENTAL EUROPE:
Nilsson & Lamm, BV,
Pampuslaan 212-214,
P.O. Box 195,
1382 JS Weesp.
Fax: 31-294-415054.

For international magazine subscription orders for the periodical *Aperture*, contact Aperture International Subscription Service, P.O. Box 14, Harold Hill, Romford, RM3 8EQ, England.
Fax: 1-708-372-046.

One year: £30.00. Price subject to change. To subscribe to the periodical *Aperture* in the U.S. write Aperture, P.O. Box 3000, Denville, NJ 07834.
Phone: 1-800-783-4903.
One year: $40.00.

First edition
10 9 8 7 6 5 4 3 2 1

Printed and bound in Italy